develo
strate
marke
that r

A toolkit
public li

DATE DUE			
4/3/13			

developing strategic marketing plans that really work

A toolkit for public libraries

Terry Kendrick

facet publishing

© Terry Kendrick 2006

Published by
Facet Publishing
7 Ridgmount Street
London WC1E 7AE
www.facetpublishing.co.uk

Facet Publishing is wholly owned by CILIP: the Chartered Institute of Library and Information Professionals.

First published 2006

British Library Cataloguing in Publication Data
A catalogue record for this book is available from the British Library.

ISBN-13: 978-1-85604-548-X
ISBN-10: 1-85604-548-3

Typeset in 11/15 pt University Old Style and Zurich Expanded by Facet Publishing.
Printed and made in Great Britain by MPG Books Ltd, Bodmin, Cornwall.

Contents

Acknowledgements

Every book is influenced by a whole range of people, ideas and events. This book is certainly no exception. There are three types of acknowledgement which need to be made: a hat tipped to those colleagues in marketing I have had the pleasure to have worked with on projects in 17 countries for over 50 large organizations since 1986; a curtain call for all those public and other librarians who I have worked for and with since 1973; and a debt of gratitude for those who kept me moving on with the book when my attention was wavering.

First, many of the ideas adapted in this book for public libraries originally came to me when travelling the world undertaking marketing planning consultancy and training. Very influential in my thinking have been two travelling partners from Cranfield University – Professor Malcolm McDonald and Richard Yallop. Both are truly inspirational in days when inspiration is at a premium.

Second, many of the ideas in this book have been tested in training and consultancy sessions for public librarians. From my employed days I owe thanks to colleagues from public libraries in Gloucestershire, Northumberland, Norfolk and Essex. In my consultancy and training activities many public library staff in the UK, both professional and support staff, have heard my musings on aspects of marketing and it should be acknowledged here that their challenges and insights have in turn influenced my thinking. This has hopefully ensured that I write within the context of what is possible for public libraries, not in some abstract sense of what is ideal. Special mention should be made here of Jennifer Holland, Head of Libraries, Norfolk County Council, who candidly discussed with me how marketing planning had been undertaken for the flagship Forum in Norwich. In addition, Penny Simmonds at CILIP has, over a number of years, shown a commitment to providing me with a training platform to introduce or reinforce marketing ideas within the profession.

Finally, ideas are of no use to a book unless they hit the page. Here Gilly Cunningham must be mentioned for her good humour, 'gentle' persuasion when my attention wandered, and the ability to present coffee at just the right time. Hopefully the regular sound of Peter Green's blue guitar and the view from my study window have influenced my writing style to make the book read easily as well as offer helpful ideas.

Introduction

While tactical marketing programmes are now commonplace in public libraries it is only recently that strategic marketing plans have become evident within library authorities. A quick glimpse at library and other websites in, for example, Australia, New Zealand, the USA, Scandinavia and the UK will reveal a wealth of advertising and promotional campaigns, some of which are isolated programmes but others which are clearly part of an unfolding marketing strategy and plan.

The author's experience of running marketing planning workshops for libraries, both as open workshops and as part of consultancy activity, is that there is much interest in planning marketing as a strategic exercise rather than simply a series of unconnected advertising and promotional activities. In addition, governments around the world are building marketing planning techniques into the way they approach the provision of public library services, and it is clear that local authorities are expected to commit more effort to marketing strategies and plans within such national frameworks.

This book is for those taking this journey from disconnected marketing programmes to integrated marketing plans. Many of the tools and techniques in this book are adapted from traditional private sector strategic and marketing planning approaches, but the reader should not feel that this is yet another case of business tools being foisted upon public services whose values and expected outcomes or impacts are not totally comparable with the expectations of the private sector. The author spent 10 years in public library authorities before becoming a freelance marketing consultant for the past 20 years working for over 50 large organizations (private and public sector) in 17 different countries. The public library planning context is, in many ways, very different from that of business, yet both seek profit – one seeks financial profit for shareholders; the other seeks profit as social capital, community cohesion or inclusion within community for its stakeholders. For both it is possible to 'get lucky', but some degree of marketing planning is likely to help deliver the benefits they seek to acquire or distribute to shareholders or stakeholders.

This book is for all levels of library management: marketing planning is an inclusive process and unlikely to be successful if undertaken only at the highest level. For the senior management team this book will help structure planning, outlining the logical flow and importance of each phase as it happens. For middle and junior management there is a wealth of practical tools and techniques which, when integrated, offer powerful diagnostic and action-driven templates and approaches.

To summarize the practical aspects of marketing planning, a set of the templates offered at the end of this book is freely available online at www.facetpublishing.co.uk/strategicmarketingplans/. These will act as an easily accessible checklist of the main elements of strategic marketing planning, and offer forms for library staff to use in their own marketing planning activities.

By the end of this book you will have ways to think about strategic marketing planning for the public library. Each and every one of the tools and techniques here should help the alert public librarian develop a sound three-year marketing strategy, together with 'quick wins' to ensure energy remains in the planning exercise. These are tools and techniques that have really worked during the author's 20 years of strategic marketing planning consultancy experience. All are practical, many are simple, some benefit from reflective thought.

Chapter 1

Strategic marketing planning for public libraries: an introduction

By the end of this chapter you will have an understanding of the importance of marketing in public libraries and the challenges it faces. In addition, a strategic marketing planning process is introduced as the context for the remainder of the book.

This is a practical book for public librarians who are interested in a reflective approach to marketing their library and its services: practical in the sense that there is a bias towards action throughout, and reflective in the sense that there is nothing so practical as a good theory. Marketing theory always needs to be adapted to context if it is to underpin effectively the journey to meet objectives. This book does just that. Here you will find marketing planning made relevant for public library management and pitched at a level where the benefits of thought and actions are brought together. By the end of your journey through this book you will have gained an understanding of the marketing planning process and the key elements within it, backed by a series of templates to help you undertake planning activities and a number of examples to inspire you into action.

You are almost certainly doing marketing already

Marketing public library services is not new. Public library managers have always instinctively developed services around the needs of the community and then undertaken activities to make that community aware of the services on offer. This has been done in a number of ways, from simple activities such as creating and distributing bookmarks, to compiling and distributing new books lists, to offering events where an overview of the range of activities to be undertaken at the local library can be presented. However, despite a firm commitment to getting the message out this has been in many cases a very disjointed enterprise and, as such, an unconnected series of one-off activities. Things are changing rapidly.

In recent times opportunities have arisen to undertake more professional marketing programmes at reasonable cost and the public librarian is faced with a bewildering set of options, all of which need to be managed within a marketing plan. Advertising, radio slots, press advertising, advocacy activities, e-mail relationship marketing with existing users, direct mail for non-users, promotional activity and a host of other options exist. This book takes professional strategic marketing tools and techniques and makes them practical for public librarians keen to use what works. Most importantly, it takes this set of activities as a strategic planning exercise rather than a series of one-off marketing events. Promotional activities alone are not marketing planning, although they are a very important part of a marketing planning process.

It is time for even more professional marketing of public libraries

Most public librarians now recognize the need to market their services. There are a number of reasons why this is an important activity for the modern library manager. These reasons include:

- Significant community funds are spent on providing library services, and to maximize value from this expenditure requires that the services are well founded and communicated to those legitimate users of the service. Marketing encourages greater take-up of services and hence ensures maximum community value is created at least to meet, and hopefully exceed, government standards and performance targets.

- User needs and expectations are changing in line with their experience of contacts with other non-library organizations, in the public and private sector. Marketing is a key way to create positive experiences for users and to ensure libraries stay alert and relevant to changing needs.

- Brand and image management is very important as people tend to become involved with organizations they are happy to be associated with and feel comfortable around. Public librarians are increasingly aware of the need to reflect the right set of atmospheres and values so that users and non-users feel a close relationship between the library and their lifestyles. Marketing is the key way to develop and support image and brand, enabling these lifestyle relationships to develop in turn.

- Users are often surprised at the range of services available to them, and even basic facts about the library, for example that the service is generally free, are not always well understood. Marketing is concerned with communicating messages and building awareness over time.

- The value of libraries, though obvious to professional librarians, is not always so obvious to funding bodies or users. If librarians wait for such people to understand the benefits they offer, then development may be slower than it might have been or, indeed, it may never happen. Marketing is a way of identifying this value, developing it into an offer for users and ensuring that this value is communicated to all stakeholders. Most importantly within a strategic marketing planning context, this activity is monitored and outcomes are measured.

- Current perceptions of public libraries and public librarians may not fit the reality we wish to communicate. As the recent case of the 'librarian doll' offered by a US retailer shows, there is a potential for negative stereotyping. The small action figure was a bespectacled woman in a cardigan, long plain skirt and sensible shoes. An 'amazing push button' action moved her finger to her lips with a 'shushing action'. Marketing can counteract such stereotypes.

In summary, marketing can help inform, educate and persuade users, non-users and funding bodies of the benefits of libraries and the value they create.

The challenges of marketing public libraries

Marketing still faces some challenges in public libraries, including the following:

- Often the resources allocated to marketing are wholly inadequate for sustained campaigns and offer development. Although much can be gained from a general move towards a marketing orientation, effective marketing is based upon sustained offer development and communication around a detailed knowledge of user and non-user needs and wants. Such an ambitious programme requires ongoing commitment of resources, both financial and in staff time. Library funding is often initiative-based rather than sound and dependable.
- Some public librarians still have 'do good' views of the role of public libraries and feel that marketing will detract from this.
- The natural modesty and humility of some public librarians mean they prefer to wait for their good work to be noticed rather than shout it from the rooftops.
- There is a lack of clarity in the role libraries play in society, with the consequent lack of a strong message to communicate through marketing.
- There is a lack of marketing exposure and education among librarians.

Less talked about, but perhaps just as important, is the feeling of some librarians (though increasingly a smaller group) that marketing is a deceitful profession with practitioners who are pushy and insincere with few saving graces. Marketing is sometimes thought of as exploitative and based upon taking unfair advantage of people and situations. However, consider the qualities of a good marketing professional or salesperson – articulate, outgoing, possessing good communication skills and good knowledge of the product or service on offer, responsive to client needs, having high energy levels, willing to make an effort over and above the basic service requirement, self-confident, proactive rather than reactive, able to persevere even when discouraged. Very few librarians would not recognize these as useful, indeed vital, characteristics of the modern library practitioner.

Public libraries, certainly since the 1960s, have been keen to profess their commitment to the library user and have included the importance of the centrality of the user in library planning as one of their key tenets. Even if resource and other pressures have constrained public libraries in the effective roll-out of such policies, there is little doubt that most public librarians are in sympathy with modern marketing approaches which look for mutually 'profitable' customer relationships through a customer orientation. Some readers may be a little worried by the word 'profitable', but this should not be thought of entirely as a financial measure. For public libraries 'profit' has significance and meaning in two dimensions. First, there is the profit *to the user* in using libraries, and this is translated into value for the community. Second, there is a profit *in users for the library* – users are the source of how public libraries can meet their key performance indicators: visits, issues and enquiries. Without this 'profit' our 'shareholders', the community, funding bodies and other stakeholders, are unlikely to remain committed sources of funds for public library activities.

How can we make sense of marketing for public libraries?

Marketing is a concept that is much misunderstood, not just in libraries but also in many businesses. Often people use marketing as synonymous with advertising and promotion. While advertising and promotions are part of marketing, the marketing concept goes well beyond these two activities. A very powerful definition of marketing is provided by Malcolm McDonald, former professor of marketing strategy at Cranfield University in the UK. It is highly practical, and every word highlights key ideas which public librarians should take into account when approaching the marketing of their services:

> Marketing is a dialogue over time with specific groups of customers whose needs you understand in depth and for whom you develop an

offer with a differential advantage over the offer of competitors.
(Malcolm McDonald, *Marketing Plans*)

Let us look at this powerful definition concept by concept, and draw out the important ideas for marketing public library services.

Marketing is *a dialogue over time*. In other words, it is a two-way process which is not simply the sending out of messages from the library to users or non-users. In our everyday lives all of us are bombarded with advertising messages and slogans, many of which completely wash over us. Advertising research suggests that people now regularly destroy printed advertising material on receipt and simply do not hear television and radio advertisements in the way advertisers intended. There are a number of high-profile examples where multi-million-pound television advertisements have, in post-advertising research, been recognized as entertaining by consumers, but they are simply not able to recall the product which was being advertised. For libraries this suggests that the most effective marketing is based upon an ongoing conversation with users and non-users and not simply on expensive slogan-based marketing campaigns.

Assuming that this dialogue is in place and there are good communication channels between the users and library management, then this needs to be done, as our definition notes, 'over time'. One-off surveys of user needs, requirements and satisfaction go out of date very quickly, so good marketing practice will always collect data, not just as a snapshot but as ongoing time series data. This helps to ensure both that library management feel confident in the currency of the data and also that meaningful measurement can be made as to the effect of marketing activity over time. One-off surveys can, however, be useful when addressing specific marketing issues and where an imminent decision is to be taken which needs information support.

Let us now move on to the second part of the definition: *with specific groups of customers*. This alerts library managers to the importance of segmentation in marketing planning. To be able to create a clear, well-focused offer which can then be communicated powerfully, we need to ensure that those offers are configured around specific groups of users or potential users. Hence the need to address the next part of the definition, *whose needs you understand in depth*. There is always a danger that we will stereotype users according to single characteristics such as gender, age or ethnicity. To be able to provide a highly targeted service we really do need to look at user needs in great detail. In best practice this will almost certainly result in a segmentation of library users which will be based upon a complex mix of characteristics, maybe even including lifestyle, life stage or the benefits which users are looking for (e.g. library as trusted information provider; library as haven).

Having created a segmentation based upon a clear understanding of use and needs, marketing will then, following our definition closely, *develop an offer with a differential advantage over the offer of competitors.* In the past, library managers have not been particularly concerned with competitors but there is an increasing recognition that libraries are in a very competitive market for people's time. The internet, for example, is a significant competitor for quick reference and research enquiries. In fact, everything that a public library offers has a competitor, whether it be access to PCs (internet cafés), a quick 'fill a space' read (charity shops) or source of out-of-print titles (second-hand bookshops, the internet). A key outcome from any marketing planning activity will be to create winning offers for our users and non-users – offers which are superior to those of competitors.

So this is marketing. But why undertake marketing? What is the point of creating an ongoing dialogue with marketing communications, undertaking significant research and analysis to create a segmentation based upon user needs, and then developing and communicating a winning offer for each segment? Marketing is not just an interesting use of time: it usually will have a purpose – to create more visits, issues, enquiries or other performance-related activity. This is very important to remember because the type of outcome required will require different types of marketing activity.

Marketing planning to help public libraries prosper

Marketing is a key activity in enabling public libraries to prosper, and as such it needs to be planned, either formally or informally. Public libraries prosper by one or more of the following: increasing the number of new users who use the library; increasing the frequency of visits from existing users; increasing the amount of use when users are in the library; and increasing the length of time that users remain active members. Of course, the limited financial and staff resources at the public library's disposal mean that all of this needs to be undertaken with as little cost as possible and a keen eye trained on the political context in which the individual library operates.

Marketing activity will vary according to which of the following is the key driver for the planning period and the relative mix of required outcomes.

1   **Increasing the number of new users.** This is a classic customer-acquisition marketing activity. These new users will have no previous relationship with the library and it cannot be assumed that they know anything at all about the public library and its services. Their impressions may not reflect reality. It would also be foolish to think that non-users can naturally make the link between what the library does and what they are trying to achieve in their lives. To attract new users, marketing activities will have to start from awareness building. As we will see later, this is unlikely to have an immediate effect, and attracting new users requires a sustained marketing campaign over time.

2   **Increasing the frequency of visits from existing users.** Existing users are likely to be particularly important for developing issue figures. Marketing can help to find new opportunities for growth from within the existing user base. One way to do this is to look for ways to increase the number of times existing users come to the library with the consequent increased opportunity for influencing them to borrow more items, use the computer facilities more or whatever will help the library meet its performance targets.

3   **Increasing the amount of use (in performance measure terms) when users are in the library.** This is the core reader development role in libraries. Marketing can influence the amount of books that readers borrow when they visit. There are many ways to influence the amount of activity readers undertake when in the library, from effective display through to more proactive efforts such as checking readers have got all they were looking for when they came in. Classic

retail display techniques can potentially have a significant effect here, as can promotional activities.

4   **Increasing the length of time that users remain active users.** A major role of marketing is to develop loyalty within the user base. Having spent significant effort in attracting users into the library, it makes sense to find ways of keeping them as active users for as long as possible. There are at least two potential marketing activities here: loyalty building among existing users, and enticing lapsed users back into the library habit.

Having looked at a practical definition of marketing and considered what marketing outputs we should expect we can now turn to look at the process for marketing planning: in other words, addressing the need to put all these things together in a manageable and effective way. We have already introduced a number of marketing concepts which need supporting, and potentially conflicting, processes.

An effective marketing planning process for public libraries

An effective marketing planning process will identify what drives users and build products and services around their needs; enable a highly differentiated service, not 'one size fits all'; create value and inspiration to use the library; and do all this with as little cost as possible. It will provide a process to ensure maximum use of the public libraries by the public, attract non-users and develop loyalty behaviours in existing users, and will clearly influence attitudes towards the library – our 'offer' as the best, the winning offer (in terms of use of time) – in the scramble for their attention.

In essence, a marketing planning process in a public library service is a management balancing process to ensure that you are successful in both the users' and politicians' eyes. It balances user acquisition and retention policies. As it is a plan for the whole service one of its key roles is to make sure that any initiative you undertake does not impact adversely on other legitimate user groups. There is a need to balance the needs of all stakeholders while meeting or exceeding their performance measures (usually politicians') and expectations (usually users').

What will a marketing plan for a public library service look like? It can be as detailed or as brief as circumstances require. A plan can be 20 pages or 2 pages long. If it goes beyond 30 pages then it is unlikely to be a living document, and more time will be spent in the process of planning than actually following through the plan. It is good advice to keep it as simple as possible, while not losing the important detail relevant to an effective roll-out of the plan.

Given this advice, it is clear that the contents of a public library plan will differ according to the basis for the plan. Clearly a strategic marketing plan for the whole library service in its environment is likely to be nearer 20 pages while the tactical marketing plan for a series of events is likely to be 1 or 2 pages. However, do not over-abbreviate: 20 pages is simply a guideline. The key point is to keep it a live document that people can get to the end of without giving up.

The following are common elements in marketing plans.

Ambition, vision, mission, strategic intent

It is usual to have some statement of intent. This helps set the context for the plan. How do you know what to do if you do not know where you are trying to get to? Chapter 2 looks at this in more detail.

The market for public library services

All good marketing plans are supported by a sound and detailed inform-ation base, covering, for example, uses, potential uses, competitors, user behaviour, socio-economic/political background, technology changes and cultural factors. It is wise to include highlight data from this information base within the plan to ensure those who read the plan are convinced that your choices of strategy and action are appropriate given the marketplace public libraries operate in. However, use information sparingly in the written plan. It is important that those who read the plan can follow the logic from start to finish without having to read pages of information which are vaguely interesting but not vital to the plan. More on this is in Chapter 3.

Segmentation

One size will not fit all. Given our understanding of the marketplace derived from our research we have the opportunity to structure the users and potential users under a set of meaningful headings, which will allow us to provide distinct offers to them and, in the most developed situations, allow us to provide customization around these offers. All good marketing plans are built around some degree of segmentation, and the rest of the sections of any public library plan should be built around segments. There is a more detailed look at segmentation, its importance and how to do it, in Chapter 4.

SWOT (strengths, weaknesses, opportunities, threats) by segment

One of the most widely undertaken planning activities is to look at the strengths and weaknesses we have, and the opportunities and threats in our marketplace. At its simplest this is a short activity where ideas are brainstormed into each of the four categories. At its most complex this analysis is undertaken by segment and with models of both the competitive dimension and relative market attractiveness of each segment taken into account. The options for undertaking this important analysis are outlined as part of Chapter 5.

Objectives by segment (issues, visits, enquiries, other)

How do you know what to do if you don't know where you are trying to get to? The ambition, vision, mission or strategic intent will ensure you are moving forward broadly in line with the type of organization you want to be. The objectives by segment will ensure that your marketing activities are strong enough to deliver what you want to get as part of your plan. While the strategic intent will be described in qualitative and quantitative terms, the marketing objectives will be described exclusively in quantitative terms. When you know how many issues, visits or enquiries you are planning to generate, the choice of strategy and marketing actions becomes easier than in the absence of such data. Without this data you will be tempted into general marketing activities which may be inappropriate for the type of activity you want to generate. Issues around priorities are discussed in Chapter 5.

Strategies by segment and general strategies

In addition to strategies developed according to the targeted segment, we may also have general service-wide strategies and strategies for individual management areas such as staffing. For each segment we will need to have a clear approach to service and products, pricing, methods of contact, marketing communications and promotion. In addition to creating a mix of the traditional four Ps of marketing (product, price, place, promotion) we will need to reflect more modern marketing approaches in developing ongoing relationships with user segments. We might also consider other Ps as part of our strategy, specifically politics and partnerships, making a six P model.

A thorough discussion of developing marketing strategies for public libraries is offered in Chapter 6.

Action plan

While sitting around all day developing world-beating strategies can be a very pleasant experience, a marketing planning process requires action. The whole point of all the analytical and strategy development work is to undertake activities that attract readers and non-readers, and perhaps persuade them either to give the library a try or to use it more than they do currently. The action plan should be sufficiently strong to implement fully the marketing strategies to deliver the quantified marketing objectives (at the level set). It should be realistic given the marketplace for the public library service and our capabilities and competences, and make us the type of organization our mission, vision or strategic intent has stated. If, for instance, the objective is to increase visits by 20% over the next year, and the action plan revolves around a committee being formed to create a text for a free bookmark which is then printed and distributed widely, then think again. It is unlikely that a bookmark will have such a significant effect, although it may be a contributory factor in getting a message out.

Advice on how to develop powerful marketing communications and action plans is given in Chapter 7.

Resource requirement

Many public libraries have very limited funds for marketing activities. However, whether well supported or not, a marketing plan should clearly indicate the resources required to implement fully the actions and strategies it has developed. This is for two reasons. First, there is a need to understand what is realistically possible within the budget. Second, modern marketing is very aware of the need to justify expenditure, and when a clear understanding of cost (money and time) is in place it is possible to calculate a return on marketing investment by each marketing activity. This will help target future marketing activity. Chapter 8 discusses this further.

Creating the marketing plan is one thing; implementing it is another. In public libraries, as with many other organizations, there is a 'short-termism' which can derail even the best laid plans. There is a need to show quick wins to keep all on track. Our journey into marketing planning for public libraries will conclude, in Chapter 8, with a look at implementation issues and how to make quick progress.

What sort of process is marketing planning?

Before looking in greater detail at the elements of successful marketing planning it is wise to consider the type of process you will be undertaking. Best-practice marketing planning is not undertaken in a smoke-filled room with the objective of creating a large, profound document.

It's an inclusive team process

Marketing plans are about the interaction with real people out there who are either users or non-users. If they are non-users then they have either never been inspired to use the library (perhaps they are not even aware it exists) or have been library users and have, for some reason, lapsed. Who can help us understand this? Front-line staff will have a view on what works and what doesn't. While care needs to be taken in listening to such input, local knowledge can often explain why seemingly worthy authority-wide initiatives do not work in particular areas. Given that good marketing reflects diversity rather than expects everyone to conform to the same set of characteristics, it is vital to include input from branch and mobile library staff.

It's a set of projects in a programme

Your marketing plan will almost certainly require monitoring to ensure it rolls out as planned or is amended when appropriate. As such it needs to be project and programme managed.

It's an art rather than a scientific process

While a marketing plan is based upon both qualitative and quantitative data, it is unlikely to be a scientific process. Wherever possible, quality planning data should be used, but be aware that much public library management information is based on reporting performance measures for government, and as such, though it provides a basis for the marketing objectives, does not help with the creativity required in developing strategies to meet those objectives.

It should be a process integrated with all planning

Marketing planning is not a management cul-de-sac. Rather it should be integrated with all strategic planning and perhaps even in some cases should be the lead planning process within a library service.

It's an ongoing process not a once-per-year process

Marketing planning is a way of approaching a marketplace. It is not simply a compliance issue. If a marketing plan is written and put on the shelf until next year then it is a very expensive use of time for a limited return. The market for public library services should be monitored constantly, and the progress of the marketing plan should be a set agenda item on senior management team meetings.

It's a change process

Almost all marketing plans recommend and implement change. Standing still is not an option for most organizations, including public libraries. Change requires careful management, with close attention at all times.

It's a fun process

Marketing planning is an outward-looking activity. It is usually about growth and change. And there is nothing like the fun and satisfaction of increased issues, visits or enquiries which can be directly attributed to your marketing activities. Enjoy!

It would be foolish to claim that marketing planning is not a time-consuming process. The information within library planning management information systems is often not the type of information required for effective marketing planning. This can be discouraging, and the effort taken to collect the required information can be significant. Luckily there are strong benefits which will make this worthwhile. These include:

- focus on medium- and longer-term objectives, which can sometimes be forgotten when simply implementing the current government initiative
- a sound basis for making choices between competing activities
- structure for systematic planning which prevents 'drift'
- common ground for senior management and front-line staff.

Some may look at the range of tools and techniques offered in this book and conclude that, for their public library, advertising and promotion are all that is needed. After all, some might say that in order to improve libraries' standing we simply need to demonstrate their ability to deliver government agendas. Such a viewpoint might argue that government defines the target groups and strategies, and we simply need to get the message out. However, even here, the alert public library manager will recognise that a close understanding of the user groups and a prioritization of segments within the target groups and strategies will increase the chances of being seen as exemplary in compliance. The more reflective librarians will recognise that governments come and go, and that the underlying health of the public library needs marketing planning while current government initiatives are being implemented.

The following chapters are based on the key elements within a marketing planning process. Remember that there is no one true way to undertake this creative process. Look for the tools and techniques which add immediate value to your planning and build on 'quick wins'. Do not, under any circumstances, undertake the process in a mechanistic way.

Reflecting upon your marketing intentions:

- Are you clear about the distinction between marketing and promotions?
- Are you aware of the challenges you will face when you undertake strategic marketing planning within your library system?
- Can you meet those challenges?
- Have you agreed what the strategic marketing plan should look like for your authority?
- Can you achieve commitment to a three-year strategic marketing plan to support annual tactical marketing plans?

Chapter 2

Ambition as the basis for marketing planning

By the end of this chapter you will be aware of the importance of ambition, both qualitative and quantitative, to the development of effective strategic marketing plans. You will also have considered your overall mission and the performance indicators which will provide the desired outcome from your marketing planning effort. Finally you will have advice on how to write your statement of ambition, together with warnings about what can go wrong in crafting such a statement.

This book has a bias towards action. However, simply rushing around doing what are believed to be 'good things', with the hope that in some mystical way such initiatives will generate extra visits, issues, enquiries, website hits or other important activity which will move the library towards its performance targets, is unlikely to support effective marketing. Although it is possible to strike lucky with random marketing, it is not to be recommended as a strategy.

Effective marketing is characterized by specific marketing actions which are clearly focused on helping to achieve specific targets within a wider mission and vision, together with a set of values that inform decision making on the journey. To begin thinking about public library marketing initiatives without an idea of where you want to get to (both qualitatively and quantitatively) is likely to result in an uncoordinated approach to marketing. Marketing initiatives should be chosen for their ability to deliver the type of library activity required from the segments of the market identified to receive the marketing communications. Without a clear understanding of the level of ambition of an initiative, how will any manager know how strong marketing activity needs to be to be effective?

The degree of ambition inherent in these targets will act as a very important guide to the type, level and frequency of specific marketing communications and promotional activity. Taken in the context of the potential market for library services by segment (there is more on this in Chapter 3), ambition will set the whole tone for marketing.

Key dimensions of public library ambition

Public library ambition can be thought of as having two key dimensions:

- overall vision, mission, values, image and brand (qualitative ambition)
- key performance indicators and objectives (quantitative ambition).

Vision, mission, values, image and brand (qualitative ambition)

Vision

A public library vision will relate to local and national government initiatives together with any local factors identified, and committed to, by the library management. The vision will highlight the purpose of the public library service. In many cases this will be some combination or formulation of the well-known desire to provide for the educational, informational and recreational needs of the community through library resources and space. This vision is the context for later marketing activity. In essence the vision is a mental image of a possible future desirable state of the public library service, which may or may not be fully achieved, but which is a reasonable and relevant aspiration to use as the guide to mission and marketing and performance objectives.

Mission

There is no agreed definition of exactly what a mission statement should include. Essentially, a mission statement is a medium-term movement towards the vision, and as such will be specific enough to have an impact on the next planning period. It will not be simply aspirational but will point out some specific future states which are realistically achievable, while allowing for some flexibility. The mission will usually be an attempt to serve the general population and specific segments by fully employing the library's key and core competences.

Mission statements, quite rightly, often attract significant criticism for being so general that they have little real content. Some prefer to reformulate such statements as 'strategic intent', an intent to move in a particular direction through an emergent rather than a planned strategy. In addition, mission statements often reflect the jargon of the organization rather than anything to do with real people and customer groups. At the very least, a mission statement should say what the public library does, why it does it and what it stands for.

First question in devising a statement of mission is: whom is it for? Is the mission statement for the library authority? Staff? The public library user?

- If for the public library user, is the mission statement one that they would find acceptable? Is the service depicted in the mission statement a service they recognize and want?
- If for the staff, ask yourself: would I like to wake up every morning and know that the mission statement describes what my working life in public libraries was trying to achieve?
- If for the library authority, are all the current buzzwords in place?

Clearly there is a potential conflict here between the library authority, staff and user ambitions for the library service. For instance, for the library authority, the vocabulary of government policies may need to be reflected in the mission statement. This vocabulary may not be recognized by the library user and may prove uninspiring to the library staff. However, the concepts behind the vocabulary may be inspirational to both users and staff. Words are important. It may be necessary to have a number of mission statements which, though reflecting the difference in approach by specific stakeholders, are nevertheless broadly consistent.

Any conflict between stakeholder missions for the library service will present significant issues for the development of a co-ordinated, focused, action-driven and effective marketing plan. A marketing plan requires co-ordinated commitment to implement the mission within the vision. Try to create this co-ordinated commitment.

Values

It is possible to include a statement of the values that will guide the public library in its mission to fulfil the vision. This list of values is often preceded by a sentence such as 'in pursuing our mission we will live by the following values'. These might include people values (for example to attract and retain high-quality staff), user values (outlining positive attitudes towards users and their needs and wants), or a wider corporate social responsibility (for example to be a good neighbour in the neighbourhood, or commit to creating and maintaining a safe environment).

Image and brand

The vision, mission and values will provide the context for image and brand ambitions. Whereas the vision will often be related to political aims, the image and brand will be an opportunity to interpret this in terms of how the public library wishes to be perceived on a day-to-day basis by users.

Here are a few examples of ambitions for image and brand:

- we want to be seen as a fun and relaxed place to visit
- we want to be seen as the heart of the community
- we want to be the first thing that comes to mind when a member of our community needs information of any sort.

At this point it is important to recognize that any later brand building will require this to be within the clearly stated vision, mission, values and strategic intent.

Key performance indicators and objectives (quantitative ambition)

In addition to the generalized mission, vision and values statement, public library ambition is very much described by its performance measures and indicators. It is commendable to have a vision of the future, a clear idea of the mission on and a statement of the values the library will be managed by along the journey to public library heaven. But how will progress be measured?

As well as some formulation of vision, mission and values, a public library ambition needs to have a quantified set of objectives if it is to formulate a sound strategic marketing plan. How many issues, by when? How many visits, by when? How many website hits, by when? Without some degree of understanding of the levels of return on marketing investment to be achieved, it is almost impossible to devise an effective and persuasive marketing plan.

What does this mean in practice? Well, consider three possible quantified ambitions by a public library authority currently reporting 200,000 visits per year in an area where there is potential for 500,000 visits per year:

- scenario 1: maintain visit levels at 200,000
- scenario 2: increase visit levels to 300,000
- scenario 3: increase visit levels to 500,000.

First, does it seem strange that we are introducing quantified ambition so early in the marketing process? Should not the marketing plan simply begin with a qualitative statement of mission vision and values? Well, the most important thing is to create highly targeted marketing – marketing targeted at specific user segments or pockets of potential use (visits, issues, etc.). The 'size of the prize' is one important factor in identifying where attention should be focused.

If there is an intention simply to increase visits by 50% (scenario 2), this will require a different marketing strategy plan and resource than will an intention to more than double visits (scenario 3). Hence the importance of a quantified ambition in support of the qualitative vision, mission and values. How does a library manager know what marketing activity to choose if he or she does not know what level of growth is intended? Marketing activities are not intrinsically good or bad in themselves, but become so in terms of how appropriate they are to achieve specific aims – qualitatively and quantitatively. With this top-level ambition in place a set of strategies can be created to meet specific marketing objectives by segment. This will be developed in Chapter 6.

A public library marketing plan is a plan to do something. It is very much action driven, based on a deep understanding of the user groups to be served and the developing competences of the service to meet and service those needs.

But if it is a plan to *do* something, then what exactly is that something supposed to achieve? And is the final state to be achieved clear enough to make the journey comprehensible to all key stakeholders, including the library authority, the library staff and the library users?

The public library marketing plan can achieve the degree of focus it needs to be actionable and effective only if there is a clear, shared understanding of the ambition of the service. The strategic marketing plan will take the ambition and provide the roadmap for the next three years of working towards that ambition. A supporting one-year action plan (year one detailed implementation of the three-year plan) will provide the specific actions needed to get the process moving forward.

The marketing plan is the overarching structure for the commitment to deliver the value inherent in the ambition. It naturally follows that, to achieve that value, all marketing activity should be united around a strategic intent which has a clear, not vague, ambition.

How to write a statement of ambition for your public library

An effective statement of ambition combines qualitative and quantitative elements and:

* is best developed with input from all levels of staff, led by the senior management team and with commitment from the library committee membership
* is not so long as to confuse the context for marketing planning, and

not too short as to be glib or like a slogan (e.g. the slogan, 'we aim to help people have more fulfilling lives' sets the atmosphere, and can be very useful to attract attention if well devised, but it does not provide the practical basis for realistic short- to medium-term planning)

- relates to your specific public library service and is not just an amalgam of other library mission statements simply with different quantitative data!

Use the template in Figure 2.1 to gather your ideas on your ambition. While there is no ideal size for a statement of ambition, it should be succinct. It can be a challenge to provide a picture of ambition both in terms of vision, mission, values and quantitative objectives. Avoid 'big mistakes'. When writing a statement of ambition it is a big mistake if:

- one person writes it – you may be able to write it yourself but you won't be able to deliver it on your own, no matter how good a public library leader and manager you are
- you try to please everyone with one statement; for example, using words that local politicians will understand, but staff and users have no idea about. There are different types of stakeholder. If you need to reflect different vocabularies then you need to write a series of consistent

Vision: What? The picture of the future we hope to create	
Mission: How will we move towards the vision in the medium term?	
Values: How do we want to act, consistent with our mission, along the path toward achieving our vision?	
Quantified ambition: Issues, visits, enquiries, etc., now and in three years' time	

Figure 2.1   Statement of ambition

statements to reflect these differences. This is perfectly acceptable in the process of creating ambition and reflects a key marketing concept – segmentation. Each stakeholder group will have slightly different reasonable expectations of the public library, and each should be in no doubt as to where you are taking the library service *in their terms*.

'Big mistakes' when devising quantified objectives include:

- not being clear which user groups are likely to support the achievement of the quantified objectives
- having unrealistic expectations – many marketing activities will not deliver immediate results, but will do so over a period of several years if sustained
- having no idea of what has worked in the past, and how well. Although the future will not be the same as the past, it is very useful to have an indication of the amount of return received for specific types of past marketing activity; this will help to set realistic expectations in the plan. In some marketing planning, such as customer retention activities, it soon becomes evident what will work and what will not.

When it has been written, challenge the statement of ambition:

- Can you see how it directly links to what you should do next? In other words, does it provide a practical context for your forthcoming marketing plan? If it feels over-generalized then it is likely not only that staff will be unconvinced, but also that you will not be able to create a crisp, inspiring marketing plan which unites the staff in pursuit of your ambition.
- Would all stakeholders understand it, feel inspired by it and get behind it? If you feel this would vary between stakeholders, then consider writing separate, consistent, ambitions for each. Marketing is about communicating messages as much as it is about anything, and if you need to create different messages to different stakeholder groups then just do that.
- Does it create a 'buzz'? Can that 'buzz' be marketed and communicated? Don't forget, for marketing planning you should be making use of the

mission statement, not just presenting it to the library committee and maybe putting it on the wall.

- Is the ambition likely to sustain activities for at least two strategic planning periods (e.g. six years?). Given the inevitable amount of change that library markets experience, will it still look appropriate in five years' time? Can it remain a unifying force for staff through the inevitable changes in customer and other stakeholder needs and expectations?
- Will it survive the changing government initiatives?
- Will it survive the legitimate distractions posed by library committee members with specific agendas?

In summary, is it succinct, exciting, believable, robust and achievable?

Writing a marketing plan is likely to be little more than an advertising and promotional plan if you:

- do not know what your public library stands for and believes in
- do not know the principles you operate from and how you will treat those who come in contact with the public library
- are not excited about what you are doing and lack a passion for your public library service provision
- are out of touch with your customers and the feelings of your own employees and library authority members
- have little grasp of the performance metrics and how they have been influenced by specific marketing initiatives in the past.

Do not expect to feel that you have to get it completely right at the beginning of your marketing planning process. Initially spend no more than a half day on creating the ambition – you may well want to change it as the marketing planning for your library plays out. It is not unusual for an initial statement to prove over-optimistic when later research shows either a smaller size of library market than originally envisaged or a more difficult market to crack than first assumed. Marketing planning is an iterative process.

Figure 2.2 illustrates the central importance of a statement of ambition to the marketing plan. General mission, vision and values, together with local and central government policies (both specifically for libraries and more generally for social and economic development), provide an important context for strategic marketing planning. In addition, the quantified library performance expectations or requirements should be considered and documented before moving forward in the marketing planning process.

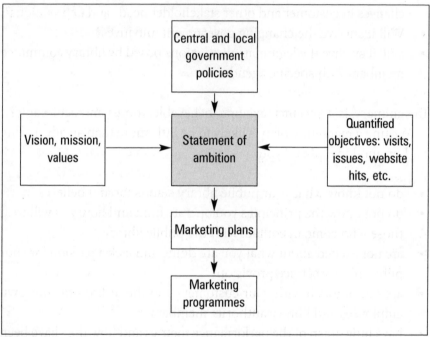

Figure 2.2   The statement of ambition as the basis for the marketing plan

Reflecting upon your public library's ambition:

- Have you a mission, vision and values statement which is a practical basis for the marketing plan, rather than being simply a motherhood statement?
- Is it succinct, exciting, believable, robust and achievable?
- Have you a quantified ambition as well as a more general statement of intention?
- Is this quantified statement clearly related to a realistic set of goals?
- Is your statement of ambition unambiguously specific to your library authority, or is it simply a summary of other library authority statements?

Chapter 3

Making sense of the market for public library services

By the end of this chapter you will appreciate the importance of defining your market, understanding existing and non-users, and using a community profile as an input into market segmentation. You will also have a set of tools and techniques to help you understand your marketplace.

Having pitched the level of ambition for the planning period it is now time to look for the people who will help the library to achieve that ambition. Marketing planners undertake significant market analysis before making choices of strategy. Textbooks sometimes refer to this as 'situation analysis' or 'environmental analysis'. Essentially this stage of marketing planning is about understanding the marketplace within which the library service operates.

A public library service is competing in a number of different markets and it is appropriate to reflect upon the markets served. For the purposes of marketing planning it is important to have a quantified estimate of the number of issues, visits, enquiries and other measures of performance to be won. In addition, to ensure that a library service has an appropriate offer in the marketplace, there is a need to create a deep understanding of what users and potential users value, need and want. Finally, there is a need to track technological, social and other changes which have a significant effect on the products and services which the library delivers or the way in which it delivers them. Market research will provide an information base to help the librarian with offer development, communication and promotion.

Without addressing such issues it is difficult to devise a realistic plan to meet clear objectives in the ambition as described in Chapter 2. With an understanding of the market for public library services (described in this chapter), we can move to segmenting the market (Chapter 4) and prioritizing strategies and actions (Chapter 5). The present chapter outlines the key things a library manager needs to take into account to ensure appropriate information input to the marketing plan. You are advised to consult several textbooks on research methodology before undertaking research into your user base. Research is inevitably time-consuming and potentially misleading unless undertaken to high standards.

Defining the marketplace

Defining the marketplace is fundamental to effective marketing planning. It is essential to have a clear definition of the market your library service is funded to serve in order to:

- Measure the library's share of the users' and non-users' activity when compared with competitors' shares. If you do not have a clear picture of the library marketplace how will you be able to define the appropriate competitive landscape in which the library operates? Undoubtedly public libraries see themselves as in some way in the marketplace for education, information and recreation, with a supporting role in other important societal concerns such as social cohesion. But what does this mean in terms of the market in which the library operates?
- Understand growth. With a very loose definition of the marketplace it may be difficult to estimate growth rates. Defining a marketplace as education, information or recreation is mind-boggling in its scope and not the basis for effective marketing planning: understanding the market as a series of sub-markets is much more pertinent. For instance,

to discuss one of the markets as providing access to the internet for 'silver surfers' enables an estimation of what, based upon demographic trends, the potential growth in this market is likely to be, with the consequent ability to judge relative priority and the return that can be expected for marketing activity and expenditure. The number of potential users who can be classified as 'silver surfers' is easily quantified and can form the basis of a quantified set of objectives, strategies and tactics.

- Identify target users or non-users. If the library market is, in effect, defined as everything to everyone, then you may have difficulty in identifying target customers which later in the marketing planning process will result in overgeneralized communications to users and non-users. There will be a tendency to provide average offers to average users, who in reality may or may not exist. Public libraries are a universal service, but this does not mean that they should be understood in terms of trying to find the perfect one-service offering which fits all. The diversity of users' perceptions of value and their consequent needs and wants should be the basis for service decisions. This may mean prioritizing by defining parts of the market which are to be served at the expense of others. Challenge yourself: 'What are we *really* in the market for?'
- Recognize relevant competitors. If you are not clear on just what market the library is competing in, then it is difficult to identify the relevant competitors to position library offers against.
- Develop marketing objectives and strategies. Without a clear definition of the market how will you know what you can reasonably expect to achieve, and what specific strategies will deliver the expected return?
- Create and implement clear marketing messages. The defined market will provide the context to any messages developed. Without a clear definition of the markets served then the mood and language of the communication may not match that of the target market.

Understanding your existing users

Later this book will be looking in greater detail at options for marketing strategy and prioritizing potential future activity. To enable this prioritization it is important, within market definition, to understand both the potential market out there to be won and the actual market already captured by the library. In business this is often referred to as balancing customer acquisition and customer retention; in public libraries this is best thought of as balancing user and non-user marketing. Non-users include both those who have never used a library before and those who have previously used the library but for some reason no longer do. The latter are lapsed users, and as such a potential source of invaluable information on how to improve the service.

This balance is fundamental to marketing planning. After all, it will be inefficient to encourage use by new user groups if at the same time existing user groups are neglected, resulting in, figuratively, water draining from the bottom of a bucket we are trying to fill. Government social agendas will often focus on sections of the public who are not traditional users of the public library service, and inevitably user acquisition has, in recent years, been the main strategy of many public library services to the detriment of user retention strategies. It is a catechism of marketing that it takes between 5 and 15 times as much effort to win a new customer than it does to keep an existing customer, and that a significant proportion of next year's activity will come from existing customers.

Any marketing planning process for public libraries which balances these two strategies will only be effective if supported by excellent quality information and insight. Public library managers instinctively know the importance of information and are naturally in sympathy with this. Market research is an increasingly important tool to help libraries achieve success. Libraries have always collected data about their users and have used this to help plan service. This chapter looks at some of the most useful tools and techniques that can be employed in understanding the marketplace for the public library.

Marketing planning, as we saw earlier, is based upon a thorough understanding of customer needs and perceptions. This does not mean that every need, desire or wish of users will inevitably be met. What it does mean is that services will be designed to be responsive to users within the resources available. Information provides one baseline from which to make decisions on resource allocation.

Market research as a source of information for your marketing plan

There are a number of key questions in public libraries which market research can help address:

- *Research into key issues.* What matters to users and non-users? Where are they going in their lives, and how can the library help them to achieve their goals?
- *Descriptive research.* What are the important characteristics of the public the library serves? What's going on? How do users access the service? When? How often? What works well for them? What doesn't? Why have some people never used the library? Why have some people stopped using the library?
- *Predictive research.* What will happen if . . .? If opening hours are changed, what will happen? What does the library have to do to attract non-users from competitors?
- *Feedback research.* How is the library doing? Are levels of satisfaction acceptable? Is the library service broadly on track or way off the pace in meeting user expectations?

From basic research in such areas the library manager can then move on to answer some of the deeper questions about creating and communicating appropriate public library service. Very quickly the more interesting questions start to appear, such as who uses what products and services, when and why? What does an appropriate collection of resources look like? How should lifestyles be reflected in the library offer?

The important point here is that research should be undertaken to answer a specific question, not simply to find out more. Information can confuse as well as illuminate. Do not add to the information mountain unless you know why you are collecting information and the specific decisions it will support at a particular time.

A marketing audit

For now let us reflect upon what is actually known about public library services. We know much already and do not want to pester users and non-users with market research surveys unless they are absolutely necessary. A marketing audit of users and non-users is required using both internal transactional information (issues, visits, enquiries and so on) and external information (demographic and other items).

A library manager needs this to align products and services into offers and value propositions for individual segments of the population. When a clear information base is established about users and non-users, the competition the library faces, and our competitive competences and capabilities (everything from products and services to buildings and staff), the library manager can begin to plan either for traditional marketing strategies (marketing mix approaches – four Ps: product, price, place, promotion) or more one-to-one customer relationship management (CRM) approaches. In reality it isn't one or the other: library managers will integrate both strategies, as this book demonstrates.

A market audit must start by reflecting upon the characteristics of users and non-users and understanding their needs and wants. In addition there is a need to understand what drives other stakeholders (library regulators, committees, staff and others) in the public library service. With an understanding of users, non-users and other stakeholders, the market audit can be completed by using traditional marketing and business planning tools and techniques such as PESTLE – analysis of political, economic, social, technological, legal and environmental factors. A thorough review of the alternatives to libraries, in other words competitors, will also need to be undertaken. This wider analysis will provide context for offer development. Offer development is the creation of an offer for a segment of users or non-users. It will be based upon elements of the marketing mix (product, price, place, promotion, politics and partnerships) together with a relationship strategy.

Who is the real customer?

As in all marketplaces, the information base should disentangle the issue of customers and consumers. The people who use the service may be the consumers, but are they the customers? Are local politicians the real customers, as they are the source of much of the funding libraries receive? In another example, who is the customer for the children's library picture-book collection? The child? Or the parent or guardian? For marketing this is an important question, as the message must communicate with the real customer while not discouraging the consumer. If this knowledge is available when strategies are developed (Chapter 6) then it is possible to create a powerful integrated mix of 'push' (directed at intermediaries) and 'pull' (directed at users or potential users) marketing communications.

An integrated marketing campaign for the children's picture-book collection would need to be based upon a detailed understanding of how issues or visits or funding is decided: one message to the customer (perhaps the parent), one message to the consumer (the child) and perhaps, where appropriate, messages to the influencers (perhaps the school). This 'decision making unit' (or DMU in sales language) should not be overlooked. Messages to only one part of this unit lose the potential to benefit from the cumulative power of integrated messaging even if they show an initial impact. Much more effective is a managed campaign to all who input into the decision. An understanding of the various DMUs that impact upon the library service should be part of any marketing planning audit. Here we are looking at the users and non-users. In the next chapter we will introduce other stakeholders.

Take some time to reflect upon what you know about your user or non-user groups and complete the template shown in Figure 3.1. You now have a list of people who need messages as part of an integrated marketing campaign when a specific product, service or offer is being marketed. Try

Library product, service or offer	Customer (person who makes the decision on the use of the library)	Consumer (person who actually uses the library)	Influencer (person who influences use of the library)

Figure 3.1   Distinguishing customers and consumers

to plan messages to all reflecting the different approaches they may take or respond to. Later in this book (Chapter 7) there is advice on how to formulate and integrate these messages.

Understanding non-users

There are two distinct types of non-users to research and understand:

- those who have never used the library
- lapsed users who, for whatever reason, no longer use the library.

It is harder to research and understand non-users than users. By their very nature non-users are less likely to be interested in contributing towards your knowledge of their lives and potential library activities. There are, however, some non-users we can call lapsed users who may be very vocal in contributing information, particularly if they are no longer users because of a bad experience with the library. These are likely to be excellent sources of actionable information, provided that the library has a commitment to change. If your glass is half empty then a complaint is a failure. If your glass is half full then a complaint is an opportunity to improve. However full your glass is, a complaint is a very valuable source of information for marketing planning. Never be put off researching lapsed users for fear of unleashing complaints. There can be perfectly good reasons for lapsed use – changes of circumstances, life stage or lifestyle. Each of these has important marketing implications for either offer development or marketing communications and is a key item of marketing information.

Many library authorities have undertaken non-user surveys and there is a good body of knowledge as to why people decline the library offer. Reasons for non-use include:

- *Lifestyle*. Given the nature of today's fragmented lifestyles many people do not find that library services fit in with how they live their lives. Commuters, for instance, may not find library services to be particularly convenient.
- *Stock*. Some potential library users do not use the library because they do not believe that the library has the type of stock they would find

useful and attractive. This may be true, but also may simply be the result of ineffective communication between library and user about stock range and availability.

- *Environment*. For some groups the library is an unattractive environment. The rules and culture discourage use, and for some groups the library is not a 'cool' place to be.
- *Access*. For some groups access can be an issue. In addition to the problems experienced by disabled people, there can be issues of access to major library collections for those who live in rural areas and have very poor public transport links. Language barriers can also be a problem.
- *Customer service*. It is not always easy to recover a user who has had a bad experience when using the library. Such users are also likely to tell all who will listen just how bad it was.

In surveys non-users also explain non-use as 'I do not read books', 'I'm not interested', 'I'm too busy and have other interests', 'I buy my own books', 'There is a lack of choice' or 'I have no need of the library'. Clearly this last selection of reasons for non-use opens up the possibilities for new marketing strategies to educate and persuade, but at this market audit stage it is important to understand just what these things mean to non-users. Is 'I'm too busy' simply reflecting that the way we deliver service is not convenient and fast enough? Is 'I buy my own books' reflecting that we are too slow on delivery, or that the library doesn't have the appropriate stock, or that the books are not conveniently delivered? Should we try to highlight the books we have that are out of print? Or is this type of reader only interested in reading new books? The answers to such questions have a real impact on the way we develop and deliver effective library services. Notice that for marketing purposes information is not just collected but is understood. Marketing information is in-depth (remember our marketing definition in Chapter 1), and the librarian needs to know not just what readers say in surveys but also what they mean by what they say.

As noted earlier, collecting user and non-user information should never be carried out on a 'nice to know' but rather on an actionable basis. The author reflects on a large-scale library perception survey (over

8000 residents) he was involved in over 20 years ago which delivered a large amount of 'nice to know' information which, when presented to the senior library management team, was so confusing as to be almost worthless, and certainly not worth all the effort expended in the data collection, analysis and reporting. Challenge any user or non-user survey you do and ask 'What does it mean if a high proportion of users answer each particular question with a particular response? What will the library *do*?' Too many user surveys collect data and then, and only then, does the library management team start to think about what it might all mean. This is not a good use of public money and is likely to promote cynicism about the importance of market research.

Good quality research is undertaken to answer specific questions rather than to 'find out more'. A good discipline at the outset of a research project is to try to formulate proposed outcomes and actions for each question. For example, 'If over 75% of people answer B to question 3, then we will . . .'. While this cannot be done for every question in a market research survey, it will focus attention on actionable information. And if you cannot formulate such statements for the potential answers to any of the questions in the survey you may find it difficult to come to any conclusions at the analysis stage of the survey.

Collecting information

Having decided what information is required, how should it be collected? Before rushing straight to a survey, public librarians should ask themselves some key questions. First, what decisions will this market research influence? Once the library manager is clear on how the information supports decision-making processes, the most appropriate tool or technique to discover the required information can be chosen. Even now, after these two important choices are made, care should still be taken with regard to quality of research. Here are a few thoughts you should consider before undertaking a survey:

- It is not always helpful in a survey to ask users what they really want. If people are simply asked what they want they will tend to want everything, and for free, or will assume that what they want is going to be too expensive for the library.

- In other instances users or non-users do not know what they want, will make up a 'wish list' and then not use the new services when you respond with specific service provision.
- With non-user surveys, sample size and frame need to be carefully chosen to avoid legitimate criticisms of representativeness. You may need to do 'snowball' sampling to achieve some degree of rigour. 'Snowball' sampling simply entails asking the few people you know who are representative of the group you are surveying if they know others like themselves. This can be a particularly appropriate approach for disadvantaged groups.
- Sometimes low-key experiments are more useful and timely than research.
- Surveys can lead to a policy of continuous improvement rather than innovation – continuous improvement, while potentially relevant for developing services for existing users, may not be enough to attract non-users or lapsed users.

How can I create the information base?

We now turn to some of the specific tools and techniques that will be among your choices: desk research, focus groups and survey research.

The choice of technique will depend upon whether the issues being researched require quantitative or qualitative data. Quantitative data is numerical data or data that has been quantified. Qualitative data is non-numerical data or data that has not been quantified. It is perfectly acceptable to collect both as part of the same research exercise.

If there is a need to count characteristics, for example to estimate market sizes for library services, then the research will need to generate quantitative data; if the requirement is to understand user perceptions, motivations, lifestyles, needs and wants, for example to develop clear library offers, research output will be qualitative data. Here are some public library examples of these types of data:

- Quantitative: age, gender, ethnicity. Regardless of what they think and believe, users and non-users possess these 'hard' characteristics. They may not be the main determinants of why individuals access libraries but they are easy classifications.
- Qualitative: expectations of library layout; reactions to a new library; satisfaction with service provision. This type of 'soft' data is based upon user expectations, feelings and perceptions. As such it is essentially qualitative in nature.

Modern marketing is particularly interested in qualitative data when deciding the range of products and services it should create and develop, and has an interest in quantitative data to measure market sizes and performance (market share and penetration) within those markets. Public libraries should likewise recognize the benefits of both types of data in library planning. The quantified information will be particularly important for evidence of performance, but the qualitative information will be the powerful basis for offer development and marketing communications. Put more simply, quantitative data will be useful to show stakeholders how well the library is discharging its responsibilities, and qualitative information will be particularly useful in getting users and non-users in through the door or onto the website or to contact the library via the telephone or mail.

What information is already available?

Here are some examples of the types of secondary desk research that public libraries may be able to collate without commissioning new field research:

- *Previous library surveys*. Although care must be taken when using past library surveys, they can be a useful starting point for your new research. The most useful previous library surveys are those which have been undertaken on a regular ongoing basis, because they provide time-series data which enables an understanding of changes in user activities or perceptions of service. One-off snapshot surveys, often on specific topics such as opening hours, have some relevance, but, unless they are very recent, are unlikely to gain the confidence of library planners.
- *Suggestion and complaint files*. Most public libraries take complaints and

suggestions very seriously and may have files of such. Care must be taken that the whole service is not distorted by one or two vociferous users.

- *National library data.* Organizations such as the Chartered Institute of Public Finance and Accountancy (CIPFA, www.cipfa.org.uk) in the UK provide very detailed benchmarking data.
- *Articles in the academic professional literature.* It is surprising just how much is already known about the way that public libraries operate in their communities. However, the public library profession does not appear to be particularly driven by such research, preferring instead to believe that the local nature of their services makes any national or international academic research of limited use in managing any one particular library system. It should be remembered that reinventing the wheel is time-consuming, expensive and pointless.

When searching for desk research data it is worth asking who is likely to need that data to be able to do their job. A quick telephone call to the appropriate person can often save many hours of research in the library. Secondary desk research is likely to be readily available and may not be particularly expensive. The limitation of desk research is that since the data was gathered by other people for other purposes, it may not be totally appropriate to the current problem the library is addressing, because of methodology or assumptions that were used in its creation. For example, library surveys, even if undertaken every year, may well reflect current and past uses rather than provide true insight into future needs and un-served users. One valuable use of secondary desk research is in the compilation of a community profile.

Community profiling

As noted earlier, good marketing of public library services is based upon a sound information base. Clearly a library manager needs to know as much about users as possible. A community profile provides the very basic building blocks of a marketing approach to public library services. Such a profile will contain very simple information about the population to be served, which can be used as a very powerful input to user segmentation (see Chapter 4).

What is a community profile and why produce one?

A community profile is a detailed description of a group of people who think of themselves as a community, and is in many cases created with their cooperation. In a library context, the basis for the profile will often be chosen not by the users themselves, but by the interests and concerns of either local government or central government. Many public libraries will already have a community profiling exercise under way to help with evaluating the introduction of various central and local government initiatives. While these will often be simply quantifications of various population characteristics, they can provide a baseline for the type of community profiling particularly useful for developing segmentation. Furthermore, this mapping of the user and potential user population can help to evaluate the success or otherwise of subsequent marketing communication activities.

Finally, there is a subtle marketing impact which can be achieved by the process of undertaking a community profiling exercise. Marketing is increasingly seen as developing relationships rather than simply sending out messages. A community profile can provide a genuine reason to make contact with local groups and organizations. This can help build trust between the community and the library service, and the community profile can be a clear indicator of the library's commitment to developing services around a full understanding of the community. However, beware that if this appears to be little more than a paper exercise, then more harm than good will be done to your marketing activities.

What should be the basis for your community profile?

As noted above, many community profiles, particularly in public libraries, will be based on local government administrative areas. A decision has to be made as to whether the basis of the community profile will be by a notional branch library area or a library catchment area. The advantage of a library catchment area is that it recognizes the reality of use for a particular library. The disadvantage is that this can often be difficult to research and may change regularly. The introduction of a new bus route, for instance, may alter the catchments of both a branch library and the central library. In many cases the community profile will be based upon a notional branch library area. This has the advantage of being useful for branch library planning and management. However, the rationale for branch locations may not have been driven by the actual way in which communities define themselves.

From a marketing point of view, there is support for the idea of supplementing library catchment area profiles with profiles of communities of interest (for instance gay or lesbian communities and specific ethnic communities) or communities of need (for example housebound communities). These profiles of communities of interest or need can be authority-wide and help ensure that small user segments are not lost within the wider service planning by branch library catchment area.

In choosing the basis for your community profile, it is wise to remember that this is not an academic exercise, but rather the creation of a practical database to help develop library services. You will almost always have some reservations about your choice as the basis for your profiling exercise. The important point in all this is to ensure that you collect useful information, not simply information that is easy to acquire.

What should go into the community profile?

There are many things you may need to know about your user and potential user population. Items of quantitative information include:

- socio-economic information: social classifications and employment patterns can be helpful in targeting services
- demographic information: age structures can help with creating the right atmospheres in libraries and ensure that the marketing communications are in the right tone of voice
- information on social deprivation: given that the mission of the public library often includes reference to improving the quality of life for individuals, a thorough understanding of social deprivation and what it means in practice for people can be a very useful part of the community profile
- housing, health and educational characteristics, which can all add useful planning detail.

Often public libraries will cease their community profiling activities when they have collected this quantitative information. However, there is an opportunity to add a degree of sophistication by supplementing this quantitative information with qualitative information. Such information might include detail on:

- lifestyles: how do people live their lives? what are the social patterns?
- life stages: having a family and retiring are two of a number of life stages which should be reflected in the way public library services are delivered
- hopes: understanding what the community hopes to achieve can provide a very useful input into the development of services
- fears: understanding what constrains the community in achieving its goals can also provide an important input into service development
- attitudes, beliefs, expectations, opinions, perceptions and feelings about life and community: these can all provide an input into planning the library service.

A simple community profile consisting entirely of quantitative data will tend to stereotype users and non-users because, as marketers have discovered, people cannot be defined solely in terms of a single characteristic. Take, for instance, age. Are all 18–25 year olds the same in the way they might relate to public library services? Well, clearly they are not, as we will see in a later chapter on segmentation. To think of these people as one group is to miss the whole point of developing and marketing effective library services. In the early 21st century, people do not necessarily 'act their age'. So age alone will not be a defining characteristic in many well configured public library services. It will, however, be a very useful characteristic as one of the descriptors of a segment. But it will be as a descriptor within a wider picture of segment and will not be a defining characteristic in itself. Of course, age might be an important way to measure service penetration in a target group of particular interest to one or more library stakeholders, but this performance measurement approach should not be confused with the more subtle approach required for marketing. There is more on this later, but for now, note that the real marketing power of a community profile is in its input to segmentation.

How do you obtain the data for the community profile?

The first thing that you need to ask when you have decided on the outline for your community profile is: has anyone collected most or any of this information already? Community profiling is undertaken by a wide variety of organizations and it is always worth while undertaking an initial sweep for previous projects. They may be out of date, but, even so, will act as good guides to the sources of information you can use.

Organizations worth contacting in search of previous work include local and national government departments, academic institutions, religious groups, health authorities, police authorities, community associations and newspapers.

Having exhausted previous work, you will have to undertake some of your own research. The quantitative data will be relatively easy, if time-consuming, to find. If you have decided to include qualitative data in your community profile, then this will be significantly harder to acquire, and will almost certainly involve you in undertaking focus groups and wider user and non-user surveys. Do not underestimate the amount of time and expertise required to undertake such activities: qualitative data acquisition should never be undertaken lightly.

When completed, a community profile is a useful resource. In summary, it will help you to:

- plan services: using such secondary data you can estimate the market size for current or proposed services and begin the process of market segmentation
- evaluate services: given an understanding of the relative proportions of particular user or potential user groups it is possible to evaluate your effectiveness in penetrating these groups and inspiring library usage
- identify resources in a community: the very act of undertaking a community profile will encourage library managers to identify information resources on, and within, their community

- develop links with organizations and communities: as part of the search for information, valuable links can be built with community gatekeepers
- create a resource for the community: the final document can be made available to the community either as a printed document or as part of the public library website – presenting this to the community can be a valuable marketing exercise in its own right
- support funding bids: given that partnerships and new sources of funding are very much the order of things in public library authorities throughout the world, the community profile can provide evidence as part of a funding bid.

Survey research

If you are looking to quantify data about any aspect of library planning which is not revealed by desk research, then a survey is an appropriate means. By the use of a representative sample of users, it is possible to make some estimations of 'take-up' for particular services or their general views on a simple issue. However, beware. These are always simply estimations, because no survey can fully take into account all of the factors which influence the user in the way they will use a public library service.

Surveys are time-consuming for library staff and intrusive into the user or non-user's day. Do not rush too quickly to a survey when you may be able to make reasonable estimates from your desk research data. If you find that the information you already have about users is either out of date or does not help with future decision making, then you may need to generate some more information through a survey.

How to undertake a survey

If a survey is found to be an appropriate way to collect the information you need for marketing planning, then take the following steps:

1 Be very clear on what problem you will be researching and the research objectives – what you want the survey to reveal. If at all possible, not only be clear about what you want it to reveal but have a view on what the results will mean before you undertake the survey. Hold your nerve with simple research objectives and if you find

yourself saying 'It would be nice to know . . .' or 'While we're asking this we might as well ask . . .', challenge yourself on how you will directly use the information. Given that public libraries are always trying to get value for money, there will be a natural tendency to look for a seemingly best-value approach to user research. More does not necessarily mean better.

2   Check that what you need to know is not already known. For instance, so many non-user surveys have now been undertaken around the world that there is a clear body of information on the reasons for non-use. Non-user surveys which start at square one without taking into account previous work are likely to provide very similar research without adding much of import for marketing planning. Remember your research activity is to support your marketing planning process, not to provide an academically rigorous information base. That is the remit of others, and there is no need to replicate this when their findings are publicly available.

3   Devise a research proposal and brief. Consider whether you will undertake this project in-house or instruct a market research agency to undertake the project. Market research is always a project and as such should be rigorously project-managed, with a lead project manager to take responsibility for successful delivery of the project's objectives within timescale and budget.

The main advantage of undertaking the process internally is that you have an understanding of what you are researching and do not have a long learning curve before productive work can begin. The disadvantage is that you may, in your knowledge, bias the project. Furthermore, given the often limited staff resources in public libraries there is the real danger that projects may not be fully implemented, completed, analysed and considered before the next initiative takes precedence.

The advantage of the external agency is that, although it initially appears a more expensive way to undertake the project, there is, in addition to its expertise, an agreed deadline to which the agency should deliver. The sole basis of its relationship with the library is to deliver in full on time. Provided that the public library delivers its part of the research process in allocating time for meetings and other agreed activities, there can be few reasons for non-completion within an agreed timescale.

Whatever approach is agreed, the research brief and proposal should include a plan with an estimate of time and other costs.

4   Choose a research method. If you intend to use an outside agency, it will be able to advise on appropriate ways to ask questions and analyse responses. Quantitative data-collection methods include postal and in-library self-completion questionnaires, telephone surveys and e-mail surveys. Qualitative methods include focus groups, depth interviews and experiments.

Postal surveys can be relatively inexpensive to administer but have the disadvantage of having a relatively small response rate. Telephone surveys are likely to have a better response, and anecdotal evidence suggests that public library surveys receive a better welcome than commercial telesales calls. Given the sensitivity of lapsed user surveys (for example one reason for lapsing is death), a gentle early evening telephone call can be the most appropriate way to research reasons for lapsed use.

E-mail surveys can be particularly useful if the group you are surveying is likely to be a particularly heavy user of such communications channels. Response rates to e-mail surveys are declining as e-mail becomes a more mainstream means of communication, but such surveys can still provide an effective channel for research activity. Public libraries can direct e-mail respondents to a hidden section of the library website where a questionnaire can be competed. It is possible to leave an open questionnaire on the website, but this suffers from the same methodological problems as noted by the in-library self-completion questionnaire below.

5   Identify the sample. Given that in most instances the public librarian is unable to undertake a census of the population (i.e. talk to each and every legitimate user or potential user of the public library service), a sample will have to suffice. Whom are you going to talk to? Some libraries undertake service-wide surveys using self-selecting self-completion questionnaires picked up from library desks. Care must be taken with such an approach as not only will they be completed almost

exclusively by users who like filling in questionnaires, but monitoring and control will have to be in place to ensure that sufficient numbers of each category of users of interest are included in the final collection of completed forms. A slightly more rigorous approach is to instruct staff to hand out forms to every sixth or tenth member of the public at particular times of day. This gives an approximation of random sampling.

One of the first questions everyone asks when confronted with sampling is 'How many people do I need to talk to?' The simple response in many organizational contexts is 'How many can we afford?', but if statistical significance is needed then there are formulae for deciding upon sample size.

There are two key concepts to take into account when identifying a statistically significant sample size: the confidence interval and the confidence level. The *confidence interval* relates to the margin of error often reported in opinion poll results in the media. For example, if you use a confidence interval of 4, and 40% of your sample picks an answer, you can be confident that if you had asked the question of the entire relevant population then between 36% (40–4) and 44% (40+4) would have picked that answer. The *confidence level* tells you how sure you can be. It is expressed as a percentage and represents how often the true percentage of the population who would pick an answer lies within the confidence interval. The 95% confidence level means you can be 95% certain; the 99% confidence level means you can be 99% certain. It is usual to accept a 95% confidence level. By combining the confidence level and the confidence interval together, you can say that you are, in the example above, 95% sure that the true percentage of the population is between 36% and 44%.

The wider the confidence interval you are willing to accept, the more certain you can be that the whole population answers would be within that range. For example, if you asked a sample of 1000 people in a city which combination of library opening hours they preferred from a list of alternative options and 60% choose option A, then you can be very certain that between 40% and 80% of all the people in the city actually do prefer that option, but you cannot be so sure that between 45% and 55% of the people in the city prefer option A.

Sample size calculators are freely available on the internet. Many market research companies mount these on their websites as a free service. Type 'sample size calculator' into your favourite search engine and you will have a selection to browse through. Here are two examples current at the time this book went to press: 'www.macorr.com/ss_calculator.htm' and 'www.rileyresearch.com/sample_calculator.htm'.

To take an illustrative example: if you want to survey an ethnic minority in your library catchment area and there are 5000 people in that category, then to be 95% confident, ±4% (an acceptable level of confidence), you would need, for statistical significance, to have responses from 375 of those people. If you received only 88 responses then you could, for instance, claim a confidence interval of only ±10% at 9% confidence level, which would be so broad as to be unsound as the sole basis for planning.

Sampling for non-user surveys can be a particularly difficult problem. By the very fact that they are non-users it is possible that you will not be able to identify where all the members of a particular group can be contacted. In such cases 'snowball' sampling is appropriate. In its simplest formulation, snowball sampling consists of identifying respondents who are then used to refer researchers on to other respondents. Snowball sampling contradicts many of the assumptions underpinning rigorous sampling but has advantages for sampling populations such as the deprived, the socially stigmatized and newly emerging lifestyle segments.

6 Before moving on to running a survey, it is important to pilot whatever survey instrument is to be used. This is to ensure that the proposed instrument will work in practice in a similar way to the way you thought it would when you sat around the table making choices. In most cases you will at find this stage that at least some small changes will need to be made to any questionnaire you have decided to use. When confident that the research will deliver understandable and useable results, you can then move on to run the research project in earnest.

7 Revise the survey instrument using the experience gained from the pilot.

8 Run the survey and collect data. If you have instructed a market

research agency to undertake this, then it will conduct the project management. However, even here you will have responsibilities to attend meetings and provide any information agreed at the beginning of the project. In addition it is always wise to ring the agency occasionally to check how things are going. If you are undertaking this project in-house, ensure that the project is managed efficiently. There are numerous books which offer help on running a market research survey and collecting data.

9 Analyse the data. Analysis should be in the context of the original research problem that prompted the project. There are a number of very useful market research software products on the market which will enable efficient analysis of market research data. These include products from such companies as SPSS (www.spss.com) and SNAP (www.snapsurvey.com). As noted above, your market research agency, if you are using one, they will have expertise to undertake this and ensure robust results.

10 Present the research results. It is now usual for market research agencies to provide research results as a PowerPoint presentation supplemented by data tables, rather than compile a full document report. It is important to keep in mind who will be receiving the research results and what they intend to do with them. Some audiences like to see detailed methodology with sample size breakdowns; others prefer top-level summaries with action points clearly derived from the data.

Qualitative information for marketing planning in public libraries

Despite the wealth of information available in a quantified community profile, there is a need to add qualitative data if we are really to understand how services should be developed and delivered. Some community profiles will naturally include such qualitative details, but it is likely that many library community profiling exercises will stop when top-level quantitative data has been collected and reported.

Qualitative data is best collected through focus groups and surveys. These can go beyond quantification to an investigation of the information needs of particular user groups: recreational interests, educational desires, information needs and their preferred ways to access services. Although these are the two most widely used ways of generating such information, there are other methods, such as observation and experiments, which in particular circumstances are more appropriate than speaking directly to users. For example, user behaviour in libraries is an ideal candidate for observational techniques, as users, if asked, may not always remember the detail of everything they have done on their library visit. In other instances a potential new service may be so beyond the current experience of library users that it may be appropriate to undertake an experiment with users to understand reactions and behaviour, rather than ask them what they think of the idea.

Focus groups

A focus group is a structured group interview with participants who are members of the target user group. In essence it is an opportunity for the library to listen to users or non-users and for users to discuss their views, perceptions, expectations and feelings about libraries. It is unusual to have a single focus group, and you may need to use a number to feel confident that the diversity of views and discussion is being represented.

Focus groups are particularly useful both in helping to identify the key questions to include in a library survey on a particular topic and also in testing the likely responses to any new initiatives or changes in the library service. They can thus be used either early or late in the research process but are not customarily a standalone exercise. A focus group will reveal consensus and diversity of opinion.

If you intend to count things – such as the proportion of fiction readers who also borrow music recordings, or the number of children who visit the children's library without a parent – as part of your research, then a focus group is not an appropriate way to deliver this part of the study. A focus group is always a non-random sample and will be based on chosen people from a target segment, and as such it will not, for instance, be a basis for scaling up a quantification of how many people are likely to respond in a particular way to any service change.

How to conduct a focus group

If a focus group is an appropriate method of data collection for your marketing planning exercise, take the following steps:

1   Remember that a focus group is a project and so needs to be project-managed. Appoint a project manager immediately you decide to use focus groups.

2   Identify an experienced moderator or facilitator whose role will be to run the focus group and report back on the proceedings. The moderator or facilitator should be skilled in managing group interactions. While it is possible to use an existing member of library staff to undertake this role, do not underestimate the value of a trained professional to tease out important information. It is not simply a matter of having an outgoing personality, but also requires an ability to bring out all points of view from all attendees, some of whom may be more reticent than others. Another disadvantage of using a member of library staff as a moderator or facilitator is that there is a potential for leading questions to be asked rather than more open discussion. Of course, library staff should be heavily involved in setting up the topic guide for the focus group and should fully brief the moderator or facilitator on the meaning of some of the key concepts.

3   Ensure that the project manager co-ordinates the key ideas, questions or issues to be put before the focus group attendees, and in conjunction with the moderator of facilitator agrees the topic guide. Here are some example areas where a focus group would provide particularly useful data, insights and opinions:

–   reaction to potential new services
–   reaction to recently introduced new services
–   experience of library guiding
–   feelings when visiting the library
–   clarification of the results of surveys.

Notice that focus groups are particularly valuable when addressing how people feel about the library and its services or where their opinions are important, such as in the early stages of designing a new library building, or where there are two ways in which the library could go, and reaction to the alternatives is potentially useful before a final decision is made. Focus groups can be built around possible futures or reflection on just how services have rolled out in practice for the user group. Most importantly, be sure that your focus group does indeed have focus. This method of collecting data and information should not be used to simply provide a general talking shop or for quantifying what can easily be researched from secondary sources. You should have a clear idea about how the data, once collected, will be analysed. Keep this in mind when developing the guide topics or questions for the event.

4 Identify and book an appropriate venue. This venue should have appropriate facilities and atmosphere. In most instances a *soft* area is likely to be appropriate when talking with public library users. Armchairs and sofas will facilitate a relaxed discussion within the group. Some target segments, however, may benefit from a focused group based in a *hard* area. An example would be if you were undertaking a focus group to consider developments in the business information service. A focus group of business people may prefer, and feel more comfortable, discussing their information issues around a boardroom-style table. It is appropriate to use the library as a venue provided that there is a specific area which can offer the right atmosphere and that it is likely that the potential attendees would be willing to visit the library. Some groups, particular non-users, may benefit from the event being held in a non-library venue. You may be tempted to try to get them into the library, arguing that this will expose them to its services. However, beware. Remember that the whole purpose of a focus group is to gather information to help you understand the issue you are studying, not to sell the service. Sell the service on another occasion. It is not good practice to have too many objectives for a focus group. Some focus groups will have publicity value, but do not forget their primary purpose.

5 Identify potential focus group attendees and invite them. Six to twelve participants from the target group will provide an event of sufficient size to encourage discussion. It is advisable to plan on a group of at

least ten, as often unforeseen circumstances will mean that one or more of those who have agreed to attend will drop out. A focus group of fewer than six participants is unlikely to be productive. It is appropriate to contact attendees with a reminder about a week before the group is held. Explain the importance of their views being heard at the event. It is increasingly usual to reward attendance at the event through retail vouchers or cash. There are opportunities to tailor the reward for particular groups. For instance a group of fiction readers might be rewarded by an agreed number of free book reservations.

Remember that you are not looking to reflect the whole community in one focus group. To derive useful information from such a group it is important that the group is not made up of token members who are likely to have highly conflicting views. A focus group to consider the future atmosphere within the library will not be productive if it consists of two teenagers, two senior citizens, two fiction readers, two video borrowers and two mothers of pre-school children. It would be much more appropriate to run individual focus groups for each of these or other categories of interest. You may need to conduct in excess of ten focus groups. It is extremely unlikely that one will be enough for any project.

It is also unlikely that a focus group would benefit from having users and non-users in the same focus group. The difference in experience and knowledge of the library would be too great to encourage meaningful discussion.

Potential attendees should be contacted by telephone with a confirmatory letter sent when suitability has been established and agreement to attend is evident. The use of recruiting posters in libraries can be appropriate, but care must be taken to ensure that this does not result in a self-selecting group of people whose only connection is that they enjoy attending a focus group.

6   Conduct the focus group. Welcome participants on arrival and do not forget to break the ice with refreshments. Keep the atmosphere relaxed but professional. Ensure attendees know why they are there, that they are all similar in a particular way, and the sort of outcomes expected. It is usual for the event to last between 60 and 90 minutes. Value should be obtained from the group by eliciting the whole range

of views on the issue of concern and then encouraging discussion around it. Group discussion helps individuals develop their views, and is known to encourage better recall of ideas and insight. An important role of the moderator is to draw comment from the diffident and manage the outspoken.

Consider audio-recording the event. In some contexts, particularly academic, such focus groups are videotaped, but this degree of record is rarely required for public library focus groups. However, if you decide to audio- or videotape the event do not forget to obtain sufficient permissions from the attendees. It is acceptable to use flip charts to note salient points as the event progresses. Given that audio and video equipment can suffer from such things as flat batteries, malfunction and human error in operation, it is always wise to ensure that a note taker is present.

7   Produce a report of the focus group, together with an analysis of the key topics which form the bases for the structure of the event. This need not be more than a series of bullet points, but liberal uses of non-attributed quotes from attendees is often particularly valuable. The specific words and phrases used can be very revealing and can provide the vocabulary for any subsequent surveys. Consider sharing this report with attendees. At the very least, your attendees should be offered a summary of the proceedings.

Surveys for collecting qualitative information

Although focus groups are a particularly important method of collecting qualitative information from users and non-users, such information can also be derived from the survey methodologies outlined above when we discussed obtaining quantitative information.

Given that much qualitative information is complex, it is important to use methods which go beyond simple tick-box approaches. Verbatim responses to open questions can be a very valuable source of qualitative information but it is possible to use other tools and techniques which try to model this complexity. Any good textbook on market research will provide you with a range of tools and techniques to elicit such information.

User satisfaction research

Satisfied customers are likely to tell a few of their friends of their experience, but dissatisfied customers are likely to tell even more people. Any modern public library marketing strategy will recognize the importance of customer retention, and retaining customers involves keeping users satisfied. Satisfaction will not be sufficient to develop and keep their loyalty, particularly if there are highly competitive demands on their time, but it is certainly necessary to keep them on board. Think back to your experiences of shopping and times when you have been satisfied with a product, but still bought a different one next time simply because you 'wanted a change'. However, if you had been dissatisfied you would certainly have bought another item instead, unless there was no substitute for it. Given its importance it is essential that user satisfaction is monitored.

One simple but very revealing tool which can be used either in face-to-face interviews or as the basis for a focus group is shown in Figure 3.2.

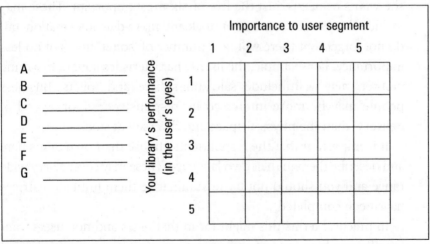

Figure 3.2   An importance/performance matrix

This matrix has two very important dimensions: 'Importance to user segment' and 'Your library's performance (in the user's eyes). If the key characteristics which the user expects of a good library service are plotted on this matrix then it is possible to get an instant picture of the overall quality of the library's offer in the user's mind. Here's how to create that picture:

1   Choose a segment or user group that you wish to study and identify individuals from within that group.

2   Identify members of the group who are to be approached to complete the matrix and decide which research method to use. A focus group or face-to-face interview is the best method to run this type of research instrument. Used as the basis for a focus group it provides a structure to allow good discussion around key requirements and performance around those requirements. It is not appropriate to use this matrix as simply another question in a general printed survey.

3   Present the matrix to users or non-users from the target group in either a focus group or face to face. Ask each respondent to identify key items that he or she looks for in a good library service, and list them in the A–G section. These are the most important things that the respondent is looking for when deciding whether or not to use library service. Do not encourage the respondent to list absolutely everything that he or she wants or needs, just the five or six most important. These may include things such as range of stock and up-to-date information, but do not forget that there will be a number of 'softer' items of no less importance. For example, the list of characteristics sought by young mothers may well include 'safe atmosphere' and 'toilets'. Business people may be more interested in 'responsiveness' or 'speed of delivery' than the physical space and diversity of stock.

It is important that the respondents choose their own items here and describe them in their own language. These may cover a very wide range and you should not try to summarize them until all matrices have been completed.

In practical terms this might mean that users and non-users want specific combinations of convenient opening hours; multi-channel access to service (static library point, access direct from home, school or work); fast, responsive service; availability of good quality resources (books, information and computers); help to access, interpret and evaluate information; and a safe, comfortable and congenial atmosphere.

However, note that there may be other characteristics which really matter to specific user or non-user segments, so do not be tempted to redefine their statements to be entirely consistent with this common-sense view of user needs. The most important information to gain is how respondents see and describe their vision of a good library service.

When these factors have been identified and listed on the survey instrument then they will have a letter of the alphabet allocated to them. In Figure 3.2 up to seven key characteristics can be allocated, to be classified A to G. If respondents can identify only four key characteristics of interest to them, then it is perfectly acceptable to simply have four: A to D. Note that these are not in any order or rank at this point. 'A' does not imply a more important characteristic than 'D'. The relative importance is considered later when the characteristics are plotted on the matrix.

4   Plot each of these letters on the matrix. The plot is derived from two co-ordinates: importance to respondents (x-axis) and library performance (y-axis).

It is usually better, though not essential, to plot the 'importance to user' dimension first. This dimension is on a scale of 1 to 5, where 1 = important, 3 = very important and 5 = critical. Note that a score of 1 does not indicate that the characteristic is unimportant: it must be important to be on the list at all. The 'critical' score of 5 should be allocated when that factor is so important to the respondent that if the library gets this wrong once it will be so noticeable to the respondent that it may well dissuade him or her from ever using the service again.

The y-axis of the plot for each characteristic is derived from the score allocated by the respondent to describe how well the library is doing in meeting that requirement. Here the 1 to 5 scale is best thought of as 1 = very poor, 3 = OK, 5 = excellent.

Take two examples of plots. First, if a respondent identifies characteristic A, 'staff knowledge of the subject', as very important, and considers that staff knowledge is excellent, then the plot is 3 by 5. Similarly, the respondent may identify characteristic B, say, 'access to staff to help me', as a little more important and a little less well delivered by the library service. A score here for B may be 4 for importance to the user and 2 for performance by the library. Figure 3.3 (overleaf) shows how these two characteristics (A and B) are plotted on the matrix.

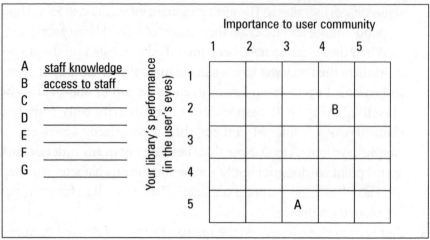

Figure 3.3   Key user requirements

5   When all characteristics have been plotted it is time to make some
     conclusions on the implications for the quality of our offer in the
     respondent's mind, a key dimension in effective marketing planning.
     To facilitate these conclusions imagine, or draw, a diagonal line on the
     completed matrix from top left (co-ordinates 1,1) to bottom right (co-
     ordinates 5,5). Why is this interesting? The line so drawn is roughly
     (this is not science but rather a way to judge relativities) where
     expectations are met. Any items which plot above this line are clearly
     areas where, for that respondent, the library underperforms. Any
     items below this line are items where, for that respondent, the library
     performs at a higher standard than is strictly necessary. This over-
     performance is to be encouraged if, and only if, there are no issues to
     deal with above the line. It is difficult to bribe users and non-users with
     more of a good thing if the most important things to them are not met
     at least to expectations.
         In Figure 3.4 with the diagonal added it is clear that the user sees
     staff knowledge to be excellent but finds it difficult to get access to staff.
     Given the relative importance of these two factors to the reader it is
     clear that investing in staff knowledge without addressing the issue
     of staff availability is unlikely to have significant impact.

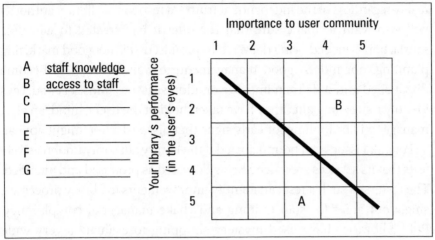

Figure 3.4   Are we meeting expectations?

Reflecting upon the set of matrices collected from respondents enables the library manager to judge whether the library is at least meeting expectations (by noting how many of the responses at least meet the diagonal line) or whether there are serious issues which must result in offer development before marketing communications can hope to deliver high levels of take-up of the library service.

Managing the set of matrices can sometimes highlight real conflicts in meeting the needs of different user and non-user segments. Making easier access for older people by having automatic doors can, for instance, conflict with the young parent's need to have a safe environment for their children: automatic doors are liable to allow children to move into non-library areas unless the children's library is a secure area within the library space. In another example, some segments may stress the need for a quiet study environment, while others may highlight the need for a more fun, vibrant atmosphere. Balancing such apparently conflicting needs and expectations is at the core of marketing planning.

Unobtrusive testing or 'mystery shopping'

No true measure of customer satisfaction will stop simply at the level of assessing user perceptions of satisfaction. Although perception is reality – in other words whatever a user thinks is the truth is likely to be their reality regardless of the independent truth – a responsible library authority will also want to make sure that the offer it has created to win user satisfaction is indeed being delivered as promised. It is not good marketing planning, nor indeed good management, to wait for users to become dissatisfied and only then improve or address issues. Most user surveys identify issues long after they have taken hold in the users' mind: an alert manager will be looking for early signs that dissatisfaction might appear.

Potential issues can be anticipated if the library authority unobtrusively tests that its services are indeed being delivered as promised and intended. The results of such a test can identify improvements to library processes, single out areas for staff training and shake managerial complacency. Public libraries have used mystery shopping to evaluate a very wide range of things, including first impressions, friendliness, helpfulness, quality of response to reference and telephone enquiries, and aspects of the physical appearance of the library.

Here's how to undertake mystery shopping:

1   Be clear on what you are intending to test and how you will reassure staff that this is not to target individual members of staff as poor performers but rather part of a process to provide a better service to the public, who justify each and every staff member's job. Furthermore, emphasize that the results will not be attributable to individuals and that the intention is to identify areas for improvement in both facilities and staff training.

2   Identify key measures and standards of whether the factors being tested are indeed being delivered as promised and intended.

3   Appoint a consultant to undertake the test or co-operate with other library authorities to test each other's services.

4   Develop a test instrument. If the mystery test is of responsiveness to users or accuracy of response, this will include questions to be asked either by telephone or face to face. If the mystery shopping is to test the facilities and atmosphere then the survey instrument is more likely to be a checklist for the researcher to reflect upon and complete while visiting the building.

5   Pilot the survey instrument.

6   Undertake the test. Mystery shopping is best undertaken as a regular
     event to identify progress or areas of concern over time. It is very
     important that the test is seen as fair and that the mystery shopper
     is not identified by staff.
7   Analyse and report.

Understanding your competition

Once you are sure that you understand the needs and wants of your users
and non-users, and, most importantly, that your offer is seen as satisfactorily
delivered, it is always worth looking at other options a user or non-user
may have in meeting those needs and wants. Competence may be a
prerequisite for winning the hearts and minds of users and potential
non-users, but it is not necessarily sufficient to ensure that they will
choose you as the way to have those needs and wants met. There is
competition out there!

Be sure to study competitive offers which your users and non-users will
be receiving. This is important information to help you decide what your
offer, or value proposition, should be. In other words what value do you
offer to the public which will encourage them to use your services, now,
and in preference to other alternatives on offer? There are some important
things to remember about value:

*   It is defined by users every day – what a librarian perceives as value
    in the library service may or may not be the same as what is perceived
    as such by library users and potential users.
*   Whether your offer, described as a value proposition (there is more
    about this in Chapter 4), is taken up will depend upon the relative value
    to the user of using you rather than one of the alternatives.

Given these important dimensions to value you can see how important
it is to understand not just user needs and wants but also what is being
offered by the competition. For each want and need be honest with
yourself. Is the library the best way for users to satisfy those needs and
wants? If not, then your marketing communications will need to be
particularly persuasive.

To begin the process of thinking about competitors consider the list of potential competitors below:

- high street book retailers
- second hand book retailers
- charity shops
- internet book retailers
- internet music downloads
- supermarket book and audiovisual sales
- newsagents
- travel shops and kiosks
- internet cafés
- websites
- internet search engines
- computers in the home
- workplace PCs
- coffee shops
- video/DVD rental outlets
- television
- music stores
- archives
- other forms of leisure, education and information
- doing nothing!

Each of these, and other competitors, brings something to the market which makes it a viable alternative to the public library service to meet the product or service need. This can be anything from better resources to a different atmosphere more in keeping with specific segments of the population. There is more on segments in Chapter 4.

Consider your locality. It will almost certainly include most, if not all, of the items in the list above, but you may well have other competitors. Who are your competitors, and why are they realistic competitors? What would you need to do to make a superior offer in the marketplace? This is key information you need for your marketing planning. Use the template in Figure 3.5 to ensure you have sufficient knowledge to underpin your thinking in later chapters of this book.

Library product, service or offer	Competitor	Competitors' strengths in this area	Competitors' weaknesses in this area	Our relative position compared with competitors'

Figure 3.5   How strong is the library offer when compared with competitor offers?

In Chapters 5 and 6 this information on competitors will be significantly improved upon to help choose priorities and strategies for realigning your offers with the marketplace and turning them into winning ones. For now, this information will help you to understand why you do particularly well or particularly badly in certain areas of service or product. Remember that competitor strengths and weaknesses should be formulated in terms of the way users or non-users would talk about this. In addition, look for strengths and weaknesses in the way they deliver specific products or services, not simply general organization-wide strengths and weaknesses which they may have.

Competitive benchmarking

A study of competitors and their offers provides useful benchmarking information which will help evaluate the potential the library offer has for success in its market. For instance in the example above, traditional reference service now has significant competition from the major search engines. If a matrix such as that in Figure 3.2 (page 55) is completed by users of the reference service and an assessment of the competitive position is superimposed upon it (i.e. competitor plots are made for each competitor and each characteristic), then a best-in-class benchmark can be identified for each characteristic. Close investigation of the best competitor in each characteristic can reveal useful improvements which can be made in the library offer.

Another way of presenting similar information is shown in Figure 3.6. Note that this, as in the matrix in Figure 3.2, can be undertaken only at the user group or segment level. It does not make sense to plot this type of information for the library service as a whole. 'Access to online', for instance, may be very important to some groups (e.g. teenagers) but relatively less important to other groups, such as general recreational fiction users. Note that this does not mean that it may not be relevant to them, but just that online access may not be a key factor in what drives them to the library. Clearly, this needs to be researched as part of the market analysis. What is clear is that each of these factors is important to a greater or lesser degree to specific groups, and averaging out importance does not reflect reality when offers are being created.

In this notional example of competitive benchmarking, the library and its key benchmark appear at first sight to be relatively similar. Both have strengths in specific aspects of service required by the user or user group. Indeed, without taking into account the relative importance of each factor it would be tempting to say that the library and its competitor are roughly equal in strength, as each is superior in three characteristics, and in one characteristic both are of equal strength. However, on reflection,

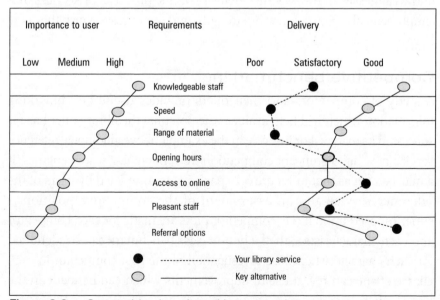

Figure 3.6   Competitive benchmarking example

the library is in a very vulnerable position. Even though it has superior access to online, pleasant staff and referral options, these are less important to the user or user group than knowledgeable staff, speed of response and range of material, in each of which the library is significantly outperformed by the key benchmark. The marketing planning implications here are clear – consider improving the offer before undertaking marketing communications. Although users are unlikely to have perfect knowledge of the options available to them, there is the opportunity to increase the chances of successful marketing.

Competition need not always be necessary. Where different organizations have similar goals, collaboration and partnerships are possible and are to be encouraged. At the market audit stage it is important to thoroughly understand needs and competitive offers in order to identify opportunities for such collaboration, or to provide the context for developing winning offers to users and potential users.

The wider planning context

Having spent a significant amount of time understanding the user and non-user, and understanding their alternatives and the competition we face, we complete this section on the market by setting the wider context for the planning period. Most, if not all, public libraries will have a context of national and local authority priorities or an agenda to which they must contribute. In addition there are other political, economic, social, technological, legislative and environmental factors (often referred to as PESTLE, as noted above) which provide a context for public library service development.

Use Figure 3.7 (overleaf) or a similar grid to consider the PESTLE influences on your users, non-users and competitors over the planning period. Will you do better than competitors as the world changes, or are you likely to be increasingly at a disadvantage? In other words, what are the implications for the library service? This completed grid provides an important data source for strategy development in Chapter 6.

Often, a planning process will start with a PESTLE analysis. However, it is better to look closely at the user and non-user base first before looking at the more general background. A PESTLE analysis in isolation is likely to provide highly general thoughts which do not connect quickly to implications for planning. However, once current needs and wants of users and non-users are understood in depth, then a PESTLE analysis can provide an excellent context for looking at how future developments in the library service can best meet user and non-users needs and wants and, most importantly, deflect competitor threats or indeed work in collaboration with competitors.

	Anticipated changes and events during planning period	Effects on user and non-user groups (does it make them more or less likely to need or use library services?)	Effects on competitors (does it make them weaker or stronger?)	Implications for library service
Political				
Economic				
Social				
Technological				
Legislative				
Environmental				

Figure 3.7   Public library PESTLE

It has hopefully become increasingly clear as this chapter has progressed that market analysis will highlight diversity and differences rather than find a neat and tidy classification of what library service should reflect. Users and non-users will exhibit a wide range of characteristics, and the competitive landscape will be complicated by specific competitors targeting various groups of users and non-users. The next chapter considers how the process of segmentation can reflect this diversity and, taking account of the market information noted in this chapter, provide the basis for effective strategy development.

Reflecting upon your library marketplace:

- Have you clearly defined the market within which your public library operates?
- Have you procedures and processes in place to ensure that you understand existing users and the way they use the library?
- Are non-users understood in similar depth?
- Have you a basic statistical profile of the community, with perhaps qualitative data as well?
- Do you understand the competitive environment in the markets in which your library has chosen to compete?
- Do you understand how your library service is going to be affected by political, economic, social, technological, legal and environmental factors during the planning period?

Chapter 4

Creating segment-specific value propositions for users and non-users

By the end of this chapter you will be aware of the need to segment your library market and have tools and techniques to help you segment and create value propositions for a variety of user segments.

As noted in the previous chapter, not all library users are the same. This is obvious but not trivial. How should this diversity be reflected in developing service offerings? Marketing planning for public libraries should recognize that any basis for segmentation is not simply of user and non-users but also of a whole range of other stakeholders. These stakeholders include local and central government and library staff. Marketing planning should take account of all stakeholder groups and segment them in an appropriate way.

For over a century public librarians have grouped users and potential users that share similar wants and needs. Although the activity has not been termed segmentation, it is in fact good instinctive segmentation for marketing planning. Groupings have been based upon materials (fiction, non-fiction, audiovisual and others), age groups (children, teenagers and adults), usage (local history, music) and need (housebound, visually impaired). In addition there are often good links with various communities of interest such as women's groups, parent–teacher organizations, youth organizations and others. These are good examples of very basic, but also very useful, segmentations, recognizing that users in each of these categories may wish to access the whole range of library services but may have a very specific set of needs that they bring to the public library service.

Segmentation in public libraries should provide the practical basis for service development. It is the process of identifying groups of users and stakeholders who have similar needs and can be made distinct offers, or who can expect distinct service packages. If this grouping is based upon their area of work (e.g. business, voluntary sector), then this is better thought of as a market sector; if based upon a complex mix of factors relating to lifestyle, age and benefits sought, for example, this is a true segment.

There is an opportunity to create a segmentation which reflects a deep understanding of user needs and requirements. This will underpin an effective marketing strategy and marketing communications programme. Breaking down the user and non-user base into meaningful segments is a difficult, yet rewarding, activity. Segmentation is an art rather than a science, and there is no one way to segment your market. It is important to look for a segmentation which will enable you to plan services better rather than simply to provide an academic or 'neat and tidy' picture of users and non-users. An effective segmentation will help the public librarian to identify and create the appropriate range of services that must be provided if the library is to be recognized by users as providing something specifically for them and not just a general service for all.

Options for segmenting library users

So how is an effective and practical segmentation developed? There are a number of bases for segmentation, as outlined in Figure 4.1 (overleaf). These options can be described as simple profiles, psychographic segmentation and, finally, behavioural segmentation.

Segmentations based on simple profiles (see right-hand branch in Figure 4.1), such as those provided by a community profiling exercise, can be useful in helping evaluate how well the library is doing compared with government expectations by client group. Clearly if the government has an agenda to support a certain age group, reporting library activities by that age group is very appropriate. Marketing may well benefit from a more sophisticated segmentation, but it is always useful to have a clear understanding of the basic demographic, socio-economic and geographic characteristics of users and non-users. There are a number of organizations which can help you to develop segmentation for your public library system. Companies such as Experian in the UK and Prizm in the USA have experience of taking huge quantities of local data and turning it into some form of segmentation.

Take an example from retail financial services to see why age alone is unlikely to be sufficient for effective segmentation. A priority group of interest to financial services companies may be, say, males between the ages of 20 and 29. However, not all men in their twenties will have the same characteristics: one may be married with children, another single and living with his parents. One may be a student with little income but large potential income, another may have a sizeable income but no potential to increase it. Integrating these criteria in the context of what

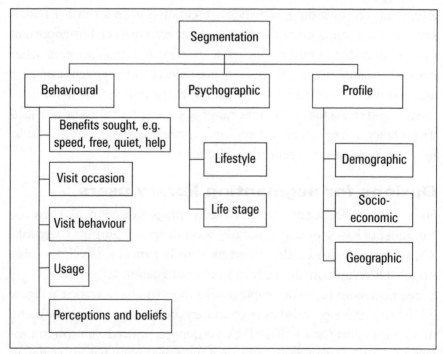

Figure 4.1   Options for segmenting library users

the financial services company is trying to do (i.e. sell) provides a useful basis for marketing strategy and communication.

Similarly, if we wish to encourage wider library use by teenagers then it becomes obvious very quickly that age alone will not be sufficient to enable us to develop a clear and compelling offer to this group. Teenagers, although all sharing the same age, have a wide variety of lifestyles and personalities. A moment's reflection will highlight differences rather than similarities. Some teenagers are studious and might be creatures of habit. We might consider these to be a segment called 'studious and settled'. Other teenagers might be significantly less studious with a much less settled lifestyle; these might be termed 'cool kids'. Even this is an oversimplification. However, what is absolutely certain is that to use 'teenagers' as a category for the provision of library services is potentially stereotyping at its worst. It is important not simply to think about the age group, but rather to investigate the whole range of needs and benefit sought and to ensure that the public library service has a clear offer covering all of these in whatever configurations particular groups respond to.

These behavioural characteristics (left-hand branch of Figure 4.1) are the basis for much market segmentation research in industry and commerce. Libraries would do well to investigate just how people relate to and use libraries. Behavioural requirements can be derived from such dimensions as visit occasion, visit behaviour, levels of usage, and perceptions and beliefs about library service. We can then sub-segment these where age, geography or other statistical profiling characteristic seems relevant. We shall look at these segments in more detail.

Lifestyle and behaviour

A study of when people actually visit the library may well reveal some important information for segmentation and marketing of library services. For example, if people only visit on a Tuesday, perhaps because a bus only comes into the centre on a Tuesday, then this is clearly a segment of library users that are unlikely to be attracted into the library on other days of the week. Simply telling these users more about the range of materials and services on offer is not necessarily going to have much impact on increasing the frequency of visits they will make. A clear understanding of their lifestyles, transport options and other factors may enable us to create a segment for which we reconfigure our offer if there are enough people within the segment to make it worthwhile. Obvious service developments would be to make more remote access options for both information and recreational uses of the library. Consequently, the marketing message we need to devise is not simply *We have this material come and use it*, but rather *We understand your needs and your lifestyle, and here is what we offer you, which is specifically created for you.* Notice that this does not necessarily mean creating whole new services, but simply making sure that the marketing messages that we send out are well focused on user 'hot buttons', rather than just a generalist message which may not inspire library use. In the absence of segmentation, it is all too easy to fall back on one message to everybody with perhaps just a little tinkering around the edges when it comes to targeting who should be sent the message.

Usage levels

Take another example – levels of usage. This is a remarkably powerful behavioural characteristic which can form the basis of a 'quick win' segmentation. Every librarian knows that readers take out varying amounts of books and make varying numbers of visits. Some readers come in every day and take out a large number of books. Others visit infrequently and take out books only occasionally. If we segment our existing users into three key groups, i.e. high use, medium use and low use, we have a useful segmentation for a 'quick win' in increasing issues. Few people would doubt that the majority of next year's book issues are likely to come from existing users. Therefore if we understood which of these are heavy users, which are medium users and which are very light users, it can focus our attention on just where the easiest increase in issues is likely to come from.

Our key marketing questions in such a segmentation are:

- Heavy: what can they offer us? What do we need to do to keep them like this?
- Medium: which of these can be developed into heavy users? What would we have to do? Also, of those that will remain medium users, how do we keep them loyal?

- Light: which of these can be developed into medium or even heavy users? What would we have to do?

If we take the very frequent users as a segment, we are dealing with people who have a relationship with the library and are likely to want both to develop that relationship and to be recognized as important customers. Current relationship marketing theory would suggest that these need to be treated differently from other groups because they are likely to be the bedrock of next year's issues. They also have viral marketing potential to spread the library message individually, based upon successful and appreciated service. Given their importance to the future of the library service, we need to understand this group in great detail. Although age may be an important factor in this segment, it may well be only one factor, and other factors may provide the basis for an effective marketing message. Everywhere consumers go they now expect to be rewarded for their loyalty. Why should it be different in the library? The high-usage patrons need to be 'locked in' to the service, and clearly there should be a different promotional campaign to this group than to non-users. This should not be seen as unequal service. All segments should have a strong offer created for them which is relentlessly communicated. But, it should be recognized that it is bad marketing practice to simply go looking for new customers without, at the same time, ensuring that existing customers are understood, valued and communicated with in a way that recognizes their previous relationship with the library. In marketing 'speak' this is known as balancing customer acquisition and customer retention.

Turning our attention now to those medium-level users: again these need a different marketing approach. What is known about them? Well, it is known that they do use the library, but not frequently. With a little bit of research it should be possible to identify a number of messages which will encourage a proportion of them to use the library more and thus become heavy users.

With the low-level users, again research should differentiate between those types of users who will inevitably remain low users because of lifestyle or other factors, and those users who can be encouraged to become significantly more frequent users.

These are just two examples of how different bases for segmentation can be relevant in developing library services and marketing messages. Your choice of segmentation should naturally arise from your understanding of your user group. You will now see that community profiling is an important first step which, with the added sophistication of benefit segmentation (segmenting the market by the types of benefits users are seeking from the library) has the potential to drive the management of library services.

Our reporting systems to government often require reporting by activity within particular age groups. While we need to report in such a way, the concept of segmentation should encourage us to plan our marketing in a more sophisticated way than just targeting age groups. Unfortunately planning mindsets are often distorted by government templates which although excellent reporting tools should not necessarily be reflected in the way we approach market segmentation. However, in recent times governments have become more amenable to the ideas of market segmentation. In England, for instance, the Museums, Libraries and Archives Council's (MLA's) marketing strategy as part of its 'Framework for the Future' has made some tentative moves this way by identifying segments with names such as 'secure families and settled suburbia' and 'prudent pensioners'.

Effective segmentation

Segmentation is not easy. To go beyond simplistic categories such as age group, gender or socio-economic classification requires a significant commitment to ongoing sensing of lifestyle and other changes which users and non-users are constantly experiencing. However, if we do not make this commitment we may find that although public libraries remain in the public's heart, they do not feature in people's daily lives. For some the public library is a destination, for others just one stop on a busy shopping trip. Library service delivery should reflect this by providing, for example, drive-by windows, online renewals and remote access to databases to which the library subscribes. All these are services which reflect the lifestyles of users. And for those highly mobile library users, access to all libraries with the same ticket is clearly a potentially attractive feature. This is becoming increasingly common.

Although effective segmentation is not easy, it can bring significant benefits. It underpins effective marketing planning, and those organizations which master segmentation are likely to have the most coherent marketing planning and marketing communications processes. Nevertheless, segmentation will reveal tensions. For example, many segmentation models will quickly highlight the problem of meeting the needs of both older people and teenagers within the same building. One conclusion may be that both atmospheres are not able to be created within that same space. A case can be made for separate buildings. In Singapore, Library@Orchard is a lifestyle library for 18 to 35-year-olds. In New Zealand, Manukau City Libraries has opened a youth library in an area with a high Maori and Polynesian youth population.

One of the most important benefits that segmentation brings is support to help us make good choices in library management. Here are some of the questions that segmentation can help the library to answer.

- *Which segments are most likely to help us to meet our objectives?* All libraries have performance measures to meet. As noted in Chapter 2, marketing planning is not an activity undertaken simply as a 'good thing' but rather as a means to an end, such as achieving some marketing objectives in library terms, often best characterized as increases in issues, visits, enquiries or other activities. Simply to undertake a generalized marketing campaign where everyone gets the same message is to assume all readers are equal. They may be equal in their entitlement to the library service, but they are unlikely to be equal in their contribution to meeting library objectives. Segmentation will enable us to identify groups most likely to deliver these objectives.

- *Which segments are most likely to use us?* A detailed understanding of user needs will reveal where our offer is most likely to be perceived as very attractive, and where it is likely to be perceived as less attractive and indeed even irrelevant. Again, there may be political reasons to market to some of those groups who do not immediately recognize or support the values inherent in public library services. Nevertheless, political reasons need to be tempered with the need to support the underlying health of the library service by ensuring high take-up levels. While public libraries are judged not simply on the implementation of government policies but also on activity dimensions such as the number of issues per year, it will remain important to identify which segments are most likely to use us and ensure that, whatever else, our marketing activity does not forget the need to configure and communicate specific offers and messages to these segments.

- *Which segments are inadequately serviced by our competitors?* Although public library services are for all, there are some areas where we provide, in marketing terms, a differential advantage over alternative ways of meeting user needs. Segments where the set of needs and benefits sought are better met by the library than by any other provider are likely to be more susceptible to library marketing communications than those segments where other alternatives to meeting their needs are noticeably better. In libraries there is the temptation, in an attempt to provide service to all, to take on competitors who are difficult to beat. For example, many public libraries have moderately successful community information collections which do not always shape up well against the range of information and expertise provided by alternative suppliers such as Citizens Advice Bureaux (UK).

Essentially, segmentation will help us identify which groups of users are most attractive to us in our quest to meet our performance targets, whether quantified or political. So how can we use segmentation? Perhaps the most important use of segmentation is as the basis for a set of value propositions.

Value propositions by segment

Why do people use public libraries? What do they value about public library services? And how does that compare with our view as public librarians of why people use public libraries, what they are getting out of it and what they truly value, compared with what we think is valuable about public library services? A value proposition describes how a library will differentiate itself from competitors to users or non-users. It is the basis for creating an offer and is defined best by what they value.

This is the heart of effective marketing. It is not enough to have a message brilliantly executed through the media if that message does not resonate with users. We need to have a value proposition for them, in other words we need to understand what it is that they value about the public library and ensure that we sell that to them, not simply our own views of what is important.

In *Management Challenges for the 21st Century* (HarperCollins), Peter Drucker noted: 'the customer never buys what the supplier sells. What is value to the customer is always something quite different from what is value or quality to the supplier'. Here Drucker is offering an important insight: what we think we are selling might not be what the customer is actually buying. This is an important marketing lesson for public librarians, and all other professionals, to learn. Are books valuable in themselves? How valuable is information? Given that effective marketing is based upon a value proposition, i.e. a set of benefits put together as an offer to a specific user group or segment, then we need to understand just what value we have to sell. It is good to have a general value proposition for the library, but nothing beats value propositions by segment if you really want to make an impact.

How does a user perceive value?

There are perhaps three main questions in the back of a user's or non-user's mind when they are making the decision as to whether or not it is worth using library services:

- Are the library services being offered to me worth the effort or price being charged?
- Do they help me to achieve things of importance to me?
- Is there a clear and compelling difference between the library's offer and other approaches to meeting my needs?

The first question noted might sound a little unusual to those public librarians who are committed to a totally free public library service. However, even where book reservations are free and there is no charge for high-level services such as online database subscriptions, there are costs involved from the user's point of view. Costs include the time it takes to visit the library, transport costs and the opportunity cost of visiting the library rather than doing something else.

This brings us to the second question. Assuming there are no significant costs in visiting the library, it is extremely important that there is a positive reason for that visit. If that visit does not help the user achieve things of value to them, then it is unlikely that advertising and promotional activity will be enough to attract them.

Finally, it may be the case that the library does indeed help the user to achieve things of importance to them and the costs associated with that are worth the effort, but that there is a better way for the user to meet their needs rather than take up the library's offer. As noted in the previous chapter, regardless of our feeling of uniqueness, reflection will identify a whole range of competitors for the user's attention. Although we may claim to have the best overall combination of services, facilities and collections to meet the generality of potential uses, once we start to develop value propositions it becomes very clear that these need to be done by segment and that the overall offer may well fall into the middle ground which may or may not really exist.

Creating a value proposition

Assuming we have positive responses to these three questions, we can start to create a value proposition for each segment of the market for public library services. As noted above, it will be fundamental for us to identify just what value is to the users because that is what we will sell in our later advertising and promotional marketing activities. To be effective marketers we may need to challenge our most basic beliefs about what value is.

Take information, for instance. Is it valuable? Can we make a strong value proposition about the library's collection of printed and non-printed sources of information? In fact, information has little or no value in itself. Information tends to have value only in use. When information is stored as a collection or subscriptions are taken out to online databases, these are best thought of as a cost, because no value is created by their simple existence. A user will not usually perceive high value in the fact that you have the material. While they may take some comfort from the fact that information is held in a free community resource, the library, real value for the user is in what that material can help them to do. It might be better to think of value in public library terms as residing in the journey that we help users make towards goals that they themselves have. Once we understand this, it becomes easy to present our services in such a way that we are clearly creating value for them. To simply inform them of the materials we have does not necessarily communicate real value, except to those who are already very aware of the library and know how to turn the collection into specific value for them. Incidentally, without this clear understanding of value, the public library will put itself at risk of potential funding cuts. A collection of data and information, for instance, has costs of maintenance and storage associated with it. Unless the value it creates is specifically understood and communicated, the collection stands out as an expensive cost which is available for cuts when times get hard.

So how do we formulate this value proposition by segment? Figure 4.2 should help you to define your value propositions. If you can complete each of these three boxes and then, most importantly, provide evidence that the value can indeed be transferred or acquired by using the library, you are well on the way to having the source material for sending a convincing message to readers – a message which will be easy to communicate and have a strong chance of attracting their attention and increasing their interest in the library, and, if it is well presented, result in greater use of the service.

When filling in these three boxes remember that the benefits users are looking for are achieved through library resources, but the resources

• Benefit user group/segment is looking for	
• Why use a library to get that?	
• Why use a library rather than an alternative? (differential benefit)	

Figure 4.2   Creating a value proposition (one or more per segment)

themselves are often not what the benefit is. For instance, a user might be looking to start a business (the benefit she is looking for), and she might use a library to help her achieve that by access to a range of excellent textbooks and referred contacts. Turning to the third box, she might prefer the library to the bookseller because the books are available on free loan; she might prefer the library to the local government business support offices because the library staff, though less knowledgeable, are very friendly and helpful. Clearly it is now possible to think about the real value of the library service to this type of user and begin to define a value proposition which can then be communicated through marketing channels.

You will see from the boxes in Figure 4.2 that the three dimensions which you as a librarian have to consider when creating the value proposition are highly related to the way in which a user thinks about value as noted in the questions above.

User perceptions of value

It is particularly important to be able to point to stories of how people have used the library, and, as a result of that use, have been able to achieve things of importance to them, hence the importance of completing the phrase 'One day — came into the library and she/he —, which enabled her/him to —'.

Examples might be:

*   One day Moira came into the library and she was shown how to use the internet, which enabled her *to communicate with her grandchildren in Australia*.
*   One day David came into the library and he saw the display of paintings by local artists, which *made the rest of his day fun and inspired*.
*   One day Elizabeth came into the library and borrowed some books on gardening, which gave her the *ideas for the stunning display of flowers in her summer garden*.

Notice that the really marketable element is in the second half of each sentence (in bold italics), not the first. Although using the internet, attending a display and borrowing some books are good outcomes from marketing, they are not of themselves the most valuable things in the user's mind. They are means to an end. Much more valuable are communicating with grandchildren, having fun and inspired days, and obtaining ideas for a stunning garden display. The alert marketer will aim to get messages such as these into any marketing communications rather than fall back on merely describing what the service has – internet, books, displays and other things. Remember, it is not what the library has that matters but how these assets help the user or non-user achieve their goal.

Try to collect stories of how users have benefited from using the library. Collect as many of these as you can. It is never a waste of time. The best advertising messages have a personal ring to them. Recommendation or testimonial is a powerful resource for developing a marketing message.

Creating personas to make segmentation data individual and vivid

Another way of utilizing segmentation data is to create personas from the stories collected from users and research data on non-users. Personas are very brief descriptions of individuals which identify 'real' human beings, similar to those we might meet in the public library or on the main street. They are not stereotypes (for instance they are not 'teenagers' or 'the retired') and should be described in sufficient detail to enable them to be recognized from a set of broad characteristics. Here are three examples of the type of information which can help form personas:

- *Margaret, age 54, part-time worker, very busy, involved in voluntary work, children have left home, interested in local history and is thinking of tracing her family tree, does not have a PC yet and keeps hearing about the internet from friends and magazines*
- *Baljinder, age 17, studying to enter higher education, very busy and gregarious, has internet at home, many friends and interests*
- *Derek, age 28, has degree but is not making progress in his career, two young children, interested in extreme sports but doesn't have time or money to indulge in them.*

Notice that they have a specific age (rather than being stereotyped as teenagers or middle-aged) and specific interests. It is also useful to include a photograph with your persona as this helps make planning more personal. Such personas can be very useful in creating appropriate product and service packages and offers. IT companies in particular regularly use personas when designing applications.

If you have segmented your market, understood the value that users in each segment are looking for and have then created a set of value propositions for each of your segments, then you have a sound basis for beginning to develop your marketing communication strategy. However, first you will need to ensure that your value propositions are not just well founded, but are also deliverable and that you have a commitment to their delivery.

Reflecting upon the importance of user segmentation:

- Have you considered alternative ways of grouping library users and non-users into segments?
- Does your segmentation reflect lifestyle, life stage and other values-based characteristics, or does it stereotype by characteristics such as age?
- Has your values-based segmentation enabled you to create a clear winning value proposition for each segment, or at least your priority segments?
- Are your value propositions based on where users and non-users are trying to get to in their lives?

Chapter 5

Priorities: making sound choices

By the end of this chapter you will have considered how to allocate marketing priorities by using a number of tools and techniques from the well-known SWOT analysis to the relative sophistication of the directional policy matrix.

Having understood the marketplace in which your public library operates and created a practical segmentation, you now need to choose how to achieve the library's ambition. Public library priorities are often set, at least in part, by local and national government, and these will form the important context for the planning period. These may include such important priorities as strengthening services to children and senior citizens, broader social initiatives (e.g. inclusion, cohesion) and commitment to encouraging and supporting lifelong learning. All of these priorities benefit from user segmentation to help identify users who might best help the public library meet the current set of priorities.

In addition, alert public library managers will look beyond priority government policies to make sure that while implementing such priorities in full the public library service does not lurch from initiative to initiative, compromising the underlying health of its relationship with existing users and potential users. An analysis of Americans' priorities for public library service in 2003 by the Marist Institute for Public Opinion found 14 priorities: reading programmes for children; open hours in the evening and at weekends; computers for public use; homework help centres; programmes for senior citizens; staff to help with computers; access to reference help by phone, fax or e-mail; access to other government services in library buildings; cultural programmes or exhibits; audiobooks on tape/CD; indexing of local newspapers; rooms for community meetings; book discussion groups; and movies or DVDs. Although these priorities were collected for the American context it is a good list from which to start and to amend when considering local priorities in other parts of the world.

Any analysis of the market for public library services will reveal many opportunities over and above those identified by local and national government. Everyone is a legitimate public library user, and the range of products and services which could be developed is limited only by the librarian's imagination. All public libraries will be working on limited marketing budgets and staffing levels which are insufficient to win all of these opportunities so, despite best intentions to serve all in full, some marketing priorities must be established. At the same time it is relatively easy to identify general strengths and weaknesses within public library operations.

Prioritization can be undertaken at a number of levels:

- by considering a general SWOT (strengths, weaknesses, opportunities and threats) analysis for the library service as a whole and building upon library strengths
- by considering a set of segment-specific SWOT analyses
- by compiling a directional policy matrix (DPM)

A general SWOT analysis

A first step in considering priorities is to undertake a general SWOT analysis. By identifying our strengths and weaknesses the library manager can estimate the relative chance of success in chasing specific opportunities. A general SWOT analysis will usually be a brainstormed four-box list of conceptual items; for example, see Figure 5.1.

Strengths	Weaknesses
High levels of awareness	Generalized services – 'one size fits all', little customization
Out-of-print titles, deleted CDs and DVDs	Lack of investment in property
Generally free	Variable stock quality and stock levels
Large number of PCs	Variable responsiveness
Heritage and tradition	Out-dated image
Truly an open community resource	Not always reflecting lifestyles
Knowledgeable staff	
Friendly staff	
Opportunities	**Threats**
Development of further IT services	Internet as a portal to information, education, recreation and culture
Inspire new user-groups to use library service	Changing lifestyles
New and multi-channel approaches to service delivery	Lapsed users may not return
	Internet search engines
Further links with public- and private-sector organizations	Resource limitations
Increased awareness of the availability of information	Changing political climate
	Falling prices for books, videos, CDs, DVDs
Support government initiatives as they arise	Confusion over role in society

Figure 5.1   An example SWOT analysis

Are you happy, as a library manager, with this type of SWOT analysis? It is clearly a very useful backdrop for creating marketing strategies. The important thing is how does the output help in setting priorities? Of itself the SWOT is, for strategic marketing planning purposes, merely interesting until it is tied down to individual segments, so this analysis should be done by segment. In Figure 5.1, for instance, internet search engines are only a threat in certain segments of the library marketplace. In addition, this type of analysis does not, of itself, identify priorities.

Prioritizing opportunities and threats

Prioritizing opportunities and threats is very important for strategic marketing planning as marketing activity will help the library make the most of its key opportunities and hopefully also make a contribution to deflecting the threats which face the service.

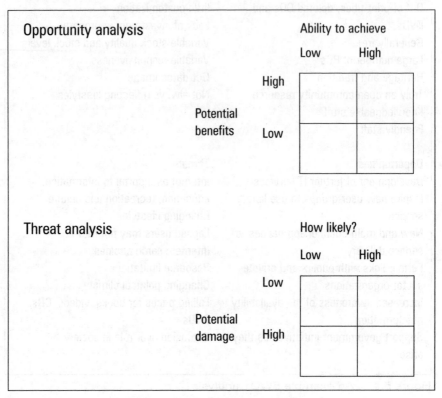

Figure 5.2   Prioritizing opportunities and threats

When thinking about opportunities and threats consider plotting them on their own four-box matrices (Figure 5.2). Such an approach recognizes that opportunities can be prioritized by each of two dimensions – potential benefits (political, issues, visits, enquiries, website hits and others) and ability to achieve (the degree to which we have appropriate competencies, capabilities and competitive advantage). Similarly, threats can be prioritized on the basis of two key dimensions: what potential damage does the threat carry if it becomes an event (how much political damage might it create or how many issues, visits or enquiries will it compromise)? And how likely is it to occur (is it very unlikely, or almost certain?)? The advantage of this approach is that it encourages the library manager to consider opportunities and threats in terms of quantifications rather than simply vague generalizations.

For instance, if new partnerships with local organizations are considered to be a potential opportunity, then 'partnerships' could be plotted in the high benefits/high ability to achieve box, with an estimate of the number of issues, visits, enquiries or other activities the partnership might generate during the planning period and beyond. Similarly, for threats, if 'internet search engines' are a major threat, then this might plot in the high damage/high likelihood box, with an estimate of the number of enquiries or visits which may be at risk. Later (see Chapter 6), a strategy can be developed to meet this threat.

Of course, for both opportunities and threats the plots and quantifications are estimates. Estimates are important in prioritization and the ability to estimate is a key management skill. It is unlikely that any public library system will feel entirely comfortable with the information base it has to quantify the opportunities and threats.

Is it enough to do a SWOT analysis for each segment? Well, that would be interesting and useful but can be improved upon. For a moment, reflect upon what you, as a library manager, are trying to do. You are trying to identify your set of options for allocating marketing effort to deliver marketing objectives which will take you some way towards achieving the public library ambition. To do this you will need to have a SWOT analysis that shows the relative opportunities (and threats) by segment, and also strengths and weaknesses relative to competitors by segment. It is obvious that a simple four-box matrix approach to such a SWOT analysis will be of great interest but is not sufficiently informative for such prioritization.

There are a number of ways to think about priorities. The simplest approach is to consider the relative amount of effort you will need to expend on existing users when compared with that on new users. How will your ambition be achieved: by developing your relationship with existing users, or by forging new contacts and relationships with new users? In reality, any marketing strategy will balance both of these. There is of course another very important category of potential users to consider – lapsed users. How much of a priority are they in the coming planning period?

Once you have a clear idea of your top-level priorities, then you must identify within each of these categories whether your priority is to get more visits, issues, enquiries, hits on the website or whatever is the basis for your ambition. Is it easier, for instance, to get visits from teenagers than it is to get book issues from this user group? Clearly there is an agenda to get people reading, but while performance indicators still insist on counting issues not simply effort towards getting issues then some hard questions have to be asked.

It is unlikely that any one campaign message will deliver issues, visits and enquiries all at once, so priorities will have to be identified and agreed so that an appropriate amount of effort can be put into developing effective strategies and action to deliver this business.

A multitude of priorities

What are your priority strategies and activities for the coming planning period? Consider the categories shown in Figure 5.3 (overleaf) and identify three key activities you could undertake to achieve each objective noted. Can you afford to deliver a positive result on each and every one of these, and other priorities (e.g. enquiries)? Unlikely, isn't it?

While this is an effective marketing approach to priorities because it is based upon the degree of relationship the library already has with users and non-users, any priority model should also be based upon, or at least take account of, a segment priority model. One such useful model is the directional policy matrix, or DPM.

The DPM is a portfolio prioritization tool, similar to the well known Boston Consulting Group's matrix. Where the Boston matrix saw relative market share and market growth as the key dimensions of portfolio analysis, the DPM recognizes that market attractiveness and relative competitive advantage are often more complex than these two dimensions, particularly when dealing not with product portfolios but with segment portfolios.

Public libraries can benefit from an adaption of the DPM, which large companies and business schools such as Cranfield University have as a core part of their marketing planning toolkits. The following adaption owes much to the Cranfield approach to this tool.

Marketing effort with existing users

To get more visits (from a chosen user segment):
1 _____
2 _____
3 _____

To get more issues (from a chosen user segment):

• increase frequency of use
1 _____
2 _____
3 _____

• increase the amount of use each time (e.g. borrowing more on each visit):
1 _____
2 _____
3 _____

To keep existing users loyal:
1 _____
2 _____
3 _____

Marketing effort with non-users

To get visits (from a chosen new user segment):
1 _____
2 _____
3 _____

To get issues (from a chosen new user segment):
1 _____
2 _____
3 _____

Getting lapsed users to use the library again:
1 _____
2 _____
3 _____

Figure 5.3   Marketing priorities

The directional policy matrix as a prioritization tool

The DPM recognizes that there is a balance between existing and new users, and asks the fundamental question: 'Where are we going to get the most return for our marketing efforts?' Taking the segments identified in the previous chapter, we can now assess their relative attractiveness to us in pursuit of library ambition and compliance with government policies. This is the regular discussion around the senior management team table when development is on the agenda. The first thoughts will always, quite rightly, turn to implementing the government agenda, but soon one will say, 'I think we should look at this group more because we can enrich their lives and expect more issues from them.' Another will say, 'Ah yes, but visits must be a priority so I think more effort should go towards this other group of readers . . . they are the potential source of most visits.' Clearly the wealth of experience on such management teams will often result in excellent priorities being set. However, such an approach also has the potential for being driven by personalities rather than a hard-headed look at what would be best for the public library service. A model is needed by which to judge first thoughts and opinions on options.

The DPM is a one-page outline of options for the future based upon the relative attractiveness to the library of each user or non-user segment. Most importantly it goes beyond a 'Where are the best opportunities for us?' approach to include, on the other dimension of the matrix, a context of 'And what's our chance of success? How attractive do we look to users and non-users?' A particular segment may look attractive, but if the library's current offer is not well aligned with their needs and wants then the apparent attractiveness is illusory in the real world of winning visits, issues and enquiries. The two dimensions of the matrix – relative segment attractiveness and relative quality of offer to the segment when compared with competitive offers – give an excellent basis for plotting segments and making strategic choices about which to develop, which to maintain, and which to remain open to but not market strongly to.

A fictional DPM with plots for four illustrative segments (both user and non-user) is shown in Figure 5.4 (overleaf). In a real-life application the library DPM would include all segments rather than the illustrative four

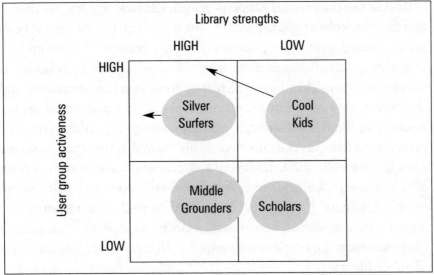

Figure 5.4   Directional policy matrix (fictional example)

here. 'All segments' means that we will be integrating both existing user segments and new non-user segments. In our example, there are four segments which plot in different positions when relative attractiveness and relative strength of offer are taken into account. 'Cool Kids' and 'Silver Surfers' are relatively attractive to the library when compared with 'Middle Grounders' and 'Scholars'. However, when the relative strength of our offer in the user's mind is considered, 'Cool Kids' in particular (and 'Scholars', to a lesser extent) do not find the library offer to be attractive. In Figure 5.4 arrows indicate the strategic portfolio shifts to make over the planning period (usually three years in marketing planning). The offer to 'Cool Kids' will involve considerable investment by the library to make it at least as attractive as their other options in the market and hopefully slightly outperform them. Also, notice that not only does the arrow move right to left it also moves upwards. This indicates that these groups are likely to get increasingly attractive to library planners by the end of the planning period. 'Silver Surfers' do not exhibit such changes (they will be neither more nor less attractive at the end of the planning period than they are now – which is relatively attractive), but the arrow shows that our offer is likely to improve slightly to them, even though it is already a very good offer indeed.

'Middle Grounders' and 'Scholars' remain relatively unattractive (notice that they are relatively unattractive, not unattractive – the language of prioritization), with one significant difference between the two groups. Our offer to 'Middle Grounders' is excellent, while that to 'Scholars' is inferior to other offers they will receive from other organizations and alternative ways of meeting a scholar's needs. The absence of arrows means that there is no strategic portfolio change expected during the planning period. This does not necessarily mean that the library does not need to undertake some marketing activities: the world and what is on offer is forever changing, so just to stand still relative to competitors means that these groups must be studied carefully and responded to appropriately. It should be stressed, as mentioned above, that relative unattractiveness does not mean unattractive. All citizens are legitimate users of public libraries.

From this diagram options for the future are clear. There are implications for relative investment in segment offers. So what does it mean if a segment falls in a particular quadrant? Here is some guidance.

1 *If a segment plots in the top-left quadrant, your user or non-user segment is one where you have a superior offer and it is a relatively attractive segment for you ('Silver Surfers' in Figure 5.4).* It is likely that these users will be prime targets for marketing and offer-development efforts. They are likely to perceive the library's offer to them as better than other ways of achieving their aims. Any marketing messages created and targeted at these segments are likely to be warmly received and understood. Effort expended here is likely, if well executed, to have both a significant chance of success and to be seen as a well-chosen expenditure of marketing resources.

2 *If a segment plots in the top-right quadrant, your user or non-user segment is one where your offer is not the best one on the market, but it is a relatively attractive segment for you ('Cool Kids' in Figure 5.4).* These will be segments where there is a great deal of potential for the library service but which need significant offer development if the library manager is to have a meaningful chance of tempting them in any great numbers to use library services. An immediate marketing campaign

to these people is unlikely to result in widespread use. There will always be some return for such a marketing campaign, particularly among those who have little conception of their alternatives, but for those who see the library as a choice rather than a necessity, a moment's reflection will tell them that there are better uses for their time with the life journey they are on.

3   *If a segment plots in the bottom-left quadrant your user or non-user segment is one where you have a superior offer, but it is a relatively less attractive segment for you than others ('Middle Grounders' in Figure 5.4).* Segments in this quadrant will usually be the core user groups of the library service. They will be segments which perceive the library offer as superior to alternative ways of meeting their needs, because it is, and for the library they may seem relatively less attractive when compared with other, more exciting, areas for development.

Beware of taking these segments for granted. Although they will appear relatively less attractive they are likely to be an important source of future activity. Marketing to these people will not be as aggressive as to segments in some other quadrants, but library strategy should be to gently remind them of services on offer and inform them of new developments. These segments are aware of the quality of the library offer and will not need to be persuaded of how the library can help them. They have worked it out for themselves in most cases.

4   *If a segment plots in the bottom-right quadrant your user or non-user segment is one where your offer is not the best one on the market and is also a less attractive segment for you than others ('Scholars' in Figure 5.4).* Think carefully before including these segments as an important part of your marketing strategy. If they are simply informed about services it is unlikely that many from this segment will rush to take up the offer. They have better alternatives. In addition, this is a relatively less attractive segment to the library than others, so why invest heavily in developments here? The return on investment is unlikely to be impressive. Sometimes it just has to be accepted that although users from such segments will not be turned away (and they will be as welcome as any other member of the public to use library services) it is not a good use of public money to market directly to such user

groups. This is not to say they will be totally forgotten – any general awareness-building campaigns will include them.

Plotting segments on the DPM

Given that the DPM is an important tool to help decision making in marketing investment, how does the library manager plot segments?

There are two ways:

- Estimate the position on the matrix. Even though this is not as rigorous a method as the second method noted below, it does bring benefits – the mindset is not just which segments are most attractive to the library, but also which segments find the library most attractive. This is important when considering how to allocate the limited amount of marketing investment available to public libraries.
- Create models for the two axes. This is significantly more rigorous, but not scientific.

Estimation is a perfectly acceptable way to undertake this exercise. Creating the models is time-consuming and will not bring great benefits for the smaller reactive library system (which should proceed directly to Chapter 6). The model-based approach is recommended only for those large reflective library authorities which are marketing planning service wide and really want to understand their strategic marketing choices in detail, applying rigour (not science, though!) to the consideration of alternatives.

Creating models to facilitate the segment plots

For those taking the model approach, two models are needed to create the plot on the DPM: a model to judge the relative attractiveness of each segment against (y-axis) and a model for judging the relative quality of the library offer to each segment compared with competitive offers (x-axis). Note that for the y-axis a model is needed which has one set of criteria (this is, in effect, the library's view of what a good segment looks like), and on the x-axis a model is needed which is personalized for each segment (as segments are different, the set of key things customers are looking for will be different by segment – if not in factors, it will be in weighting of these factors; if this were not the case then these would not be different segments).

Plotting the y-axis

We turn now to the creation of the models for these two dimensions. First, the y-axis. To create a picture of the relative attractiveness of each segment to the achievement of library ambition it is important to:

- understand what characteristics a segment should have to make it attractive to the library
- reflect current library policy in this choice
- have a scoring system to score each segment against.

Consider this y-axis model in more detail. First, have you, as a library manager, ever considered what makes one group of users more attractive to the library service than another group of users? One answer to this question would be to point to groups where the library manager believes that the library can make a significant difference to their quality of life and note these as the most attractive. This is a very important function of public services, and impact measures are beginning to be developed to act as performance measures in this area. At present, though, many performance measures are a little less sophisticated than this, and tend to be based on visits, issues and enquiries. This may or may not reflect the amount of 'good' created by public libraries, but is undeniably in the minds of funding bodies.

From the point of view of achieving our performance measures there are a number of key factors a library manager might look for in a segment to be classified as particularly attractive. These include such items as:

- number of visits received from that segment
- number of potential visits the library might receive from that segment
- number of issues made to that segment
- potential number of extra issues the library might make to that segment

- number of enquiries received from that segment
- potential extra enquiries that might be received from that segment
- number of other, non-library, providers of competing offers to that segment
- the strategic fit of the library's current asset, resources, competences and capabilities with that segment's needs, wants and expectations
- others!

Perhaps the greatest of all characteristics, though, is the potential political impact that segment may have if the library achieves a positive result with them. This is a factor on its own, but is also a significant driver in overall library policy and strategy.

It is clearly important to include current library policies and key strategies in any model of segment attractiveness. To do this requires not just a set of key characteristics and a scoring system for these but also a weighting system to reflect existing policy. For example, at one point the authority may be in a phase where increased visits are the driving performance indicator, so this needs to be weighted appropriately when segments are evaluated. At another time focus may change to increasing issues rather than visits, and the model needs to be open to a quick re-score of segment attractiveness without going back to square one.

It is usual to create weightings as scores which add up to 100. This allocation of 100 points can be easily changed if the political emphasis goes from one performance indicator to another. For example, if there were only three key factors – 'potential number of visits', 'potential number of issues' and 'potential number of enquiries' – and 'potential number of visits' was the most important factor of the three, with 'potential number of enquiries' the least important by some degree, then the weighting might be 60%, 30% and 10% respectively.

The final input to the segment attractiveness model is the creation of a scoring system. If, for instance, we use the above view of three main characteristics – visits, issues and enquiries, with a weighting 60:30:10 (that is, a current library policy based mainly on generating extra visits) – then how are we to identify the merely interesting segment in each of the characteristics, the very interesting segment and the absolutely exciting segment? A scoring system is needed which when multiplied by the policy weighting will return a score for each segment relative to each of the other segments. Provided that you are able to keep all options in your head and to centre the notional average mentally then it may be possible for you to score segments on a 1 (unattractive) to 10 (very attractive) scale without a formal scoring system. However, do not underestimate the difficulty of doing this. You may want to set some reference points for at least 0, 5, and 10, as shown in Table 5.1.

Taking these dimensions as a basis for analysis, consider the notional model shown in Table 5.1, with fictional example, for judging relative attractiveness by means of a 'formal' (but not scientific) system. Note that the factors, weights and scoring model will be different for each library authority, although it is likely that many will share a significant proportion of the factors. Weightings may be similar across authorities, but the scoring base will differ according to the size of the authority and the likely amount of activity. Note that although authorities will be of different sizes they may still have similar standards to meet.

Table 5.1   User segment attractiveness model – fictional example

	Weighting	Score		
		10	5	0
Visits potential per annum	25	>5000	3000–5000	<3000
Issues potential per annum	25	>75,000	50,000–75,000	<50,000
Strategic fit	20	High	Medium	Low
Political impact	30	High	Medium	Low
Total	100			

From the scoring model in Table 5.1 it can be seen that some factors can be easily quantified (e.g. visits and issues), but that, for some, relativities need to be estimated – high, medium or low (e.g. strategic fit and political impact). Remember that the scoring is based upon relativities and not absolutely accurate statistics. The fact that library management information systems do not provide data in this form should not deflect the library manager from making reasonable estimates in the absence of data.

Once the scoring model for the y-axis has been devised it is time to identify and evaluate all segments against the model. Table 5.2 shows a fictional example of a set of scores with segments scored against the above model (Table 5.1). (An example of how the scoring is undertaken: the score of 5 is given to Silver Surfers for visits potential, which means, using the attractiveness scoring model earlier in this chapter (Table 5.1), that this segment offers a visits potential of between 3000 and 5000 visits per annum. This visits potential factor is weighted at 25%, so the score x weighting is 5x25/100 = 1.25.)

Table 5.2   Scoring relative attractiveness – a fictional example

	Visits potential	Issues potential	Strategic fit	Political impact	Total score
Silver Surfers	5×25/100 = 1.25	5×25/100 = 1.25	7×20/100 = 1.40	6×30/100 = 1.80	5.70
Middle Grounders	5×25/100 = 1.25	6×25/100 = 1.50	7×20/100 = 1.40	2×30/100 = 0.60	4.75
Cool Kids	8×25/100 = 2.00	4×25/100 = 1.00	3×20/100 = 0.60	8×30/100 = 2.40	6.00
Scholars	3×25/100 = 0.75	4×25/100 = 1.00	4×20/100 = 0.80	2×30/100 = 0.60	3.15

At first sight it would seem obvious from Table 5.2 that some segments are more attractive to the library than others. In this chart it appears that, for different reasons, Silver Surfers and Cool Kids are the most attractive segments. Also, note that this scoring gives a plot for the y-axis of the DPM. If 'low' to 'high' is considered to be a scale from 0 to 10, then two segments plot above half way (5), and two plot below. Silver Surfers and Cool Kids plot above; Middle Grounders and Scholars plot below. Incidentally, given our use of a weighting, all total scores for segments will plot between 0 and 10.

However, beware of simply following the notionally attractive segments without reflecting on ability to attract them to library services. Notional attractiveness to the library does not mean that the library can actually deliver visits, issues or enquiries from such segments. Will the library's offer be good enough?

To balance the notional attractiveness a model needs to be created which will identify the library's chances of winning the segment's support and 'business'. People in this category may be in the market for information or leisure or education, but will the library offer in this area be the one they choose? If they want information, for instance, will they come to the library or simply throw a few words into their favourite search engine? Or ask a friend?

Plotting the x-axis

The model for judging the quality of the library offer will need to include:

- value drivers (things that matter to the users in the segment, as defined by the user) for each segment
- the relative importance of each of these drivers (weighting)
- scores for the library offer in each of these against the competition.

This will then provide the basis for the segment plot along the x-axis. If the overall library score is better than competitors', then it will plot in the 'high' library strengths position and, conversely, if competitors score higher overall than the library then the library will plot in the 'low' library strengths position. Figure 5.5 shows a chart you could complete to gain this important insight.

The chart has the three key components noted above: a space for the list of key value drivers for the segment, a weighting of the relative importance of each of these and a scoring chart which compares the public library offer with that of each major competitor. It also has a row which totals the score.

Value drivers	Weighting	Our score	Competitor A	Competitor B	Competitor C
Total	100				

Figure 5.5   Modelling the relative attractiveness of the library offer

This row will highlight the relative quality of the library offer in the things that matter to this segment when compared with the offers of competitors. When compared, the scores provide an indicator of the library's chances of success in this segment. Most importantly, by analysing the parts of the table where the library scores relatively badly, the library manager can identify key areas to improve as part of the marketing strategy.

In our fictional example above each of the four segments would need to be studied by one of these charts. It is not possible to use the same scoring system for all segments. If it were then we would not be reflecting the most important thing about segmentation – it reflects diversity, not sameness. Note, however, that for the y-axis it was possible to evaluate all segments against one model. Here we were evaluating against one view – the notional model of what makes a segment attractive to the library.

Table 5.3 takes one segment, 'Middle Grounders', to show how the x-axis analysis plot should be created (remember this analysis needs to be done for every segment). As evidenced by the 'total' row, the library has the superior overall offer to this segment and hence the plot in 'high' library strengths part of the DPM. Taking the two plots together, this segment is

Table 5.3   An analysis of the relative quality of our offer to 'Middle Grounders'

Value drivers	Weighting	Our score	Bookshops	Charity shops	Internet from home
Good range of stock	25	7×25/100 = 1.75	7×25/100 = 1.75	2×25/100 = 0.50	8×25/100 = 2.00
Ability to get materials not in stock	20	9×20/100 = 1.80	5×20/100 = 1.00	0×20/100 = 0.00	5×20/100 = 1.00
Friendly, mature atmosphere	15	8×15/100 = 1.20	8×15/100 = 1.20	3×15/100 = 0.45	5×15/100 = 0.75
Evening opening	25	8×25/100 = 2.00	3×25/100 = 0.75	0×25/100 = 0.00	10×25/100 = 2.50
Value for money	15	6×15/100 = 0.90	5×15/100 = 0.75	6×15/100 = 1.75	7×25/100 = 0.90
Total	100	7.65	5.45	2.7	7.15

firmly in the bottom left-hand box (see Figure 5.4, page 91): relatively unattractive compared with other segments (remember this does not mean unattractive), but one where the library offer is likely to be met with a positive response – a prime candidate for an 'informing' or 'reminding' communication strategy. The more complex and expensive 'persuading' strategy is not required here.

A more sophisticated way to plot this on the x-axis is to plot the library score against the best score as a ratio. If you have the best offer this will be greater than 1; if it is not the best it will be less than 1. This will enable a plot on the x-axis of the matrix, where 1 is the dividing line between high and low strength.

A close look at the scoring undertaken for each segment will highlight where our real strengths and weakness are by segment. Beware, though, that there is statistical sensitivity in the scoring. If the results look surprising then revisit the scoring to see just where there may have been overestimation or underestimation. At the very least this model will highlight just how little is known about how users and non-users think about libraries and their competitors!

With regard to the quality of the library offer, wouldn't it be great if the library had a unique offer for particular user segments? Marketers feel most comfortable when their product has a unique selling point (USP) because they can then confidently enter the selling arena with a better than average chance of winning the business. Look at the scores and try to identify where the library is unique in its offering. Is it in resources? Staff attitudes and skills? Is the library more convenient than competitors? In the modern world it is unlikely that the library manager will be able to point to USPs – there is almost always someone with an offer similar to yours! In such circumstances the library may still attract users and non-users with its offer (because they do not have perfect knowledge of all their alternatives), but to keep them loyal may be more difficult.

Reflect upon the set of x-axis segment scores and complete the template shown in Figure 5.6 (overleaf). Clearly it is unlikely that the library will have the highest score in every segment. However, this reflection should give the library manager an indication of just how strong the marketing effort will have to be to have a realistic chance of significant success. Some might say

	Segment 1	Segment 2	Segment 3
Are we a realistic player – are our scores competitive overall?			
Do we have any major weaknesses (i.e. high weightings for users where we score relatively poorly)?			
Do we have any major points of differentiation we can use as USPs?			

Figure 5.6   Competitive strengths and weaknesses by segment

that the library's real distinctive competence, from which the manager can derive a USP, is in our combination of approaches and strengths. This may well be the case in theory, but if the library manager cannot find a segment where this combination is a requirement then it is not a true differentiation in the sense that it will be a key driver of the segment's response to marketing activity.

Using the DPM plots to consider marketing strategy

Plotting the DPM has teased out the information needed to consider marketing strategy options in two very important dimensions – segment attractiveness and the chances of being perceived as having the winning offer. With this information the library manager can now plot each segment on the matrix and consider marketing strategy for each segment in the context of other segment strategy options.

In summary, the plot for both axes is created by scoring each segment and then multiplying that score by the weighting. Mathematically this means that the attractiveness score will always be between 0 and 10, the actual score of a particular segment showing its attractiveness relative to all other segments being plotted. The library strengths 'quality of offer' score will give a plot for the relative attractiveness of the library offer compared with that of competitors. If the library score is compared with the best competitive score the library manager will know, by ratio, how superior or inferior the library offer is in that segment.

There are clear strategic implications of such a plot. The most obvious one is when the library score within a segment is lower than that of competitors. The marketing strategy should, in such instances, clearly be about offer development (addressing some of the key areas within the library's overall scoring which were clearly inferior to competitive offers, yet of major importance to users) rather than simply a marketing communications campaign to inform or remind. In others, where the library offer is superior to all competitive offers, then an informing and reminding campaign is a very appropriate strategic marketing activity. If the library offer is clearly the best in the overall scoring then we should expect that when informed of it users and non-users are unlikely to find a better way of doing whatever they set out to do.

The plots are best made as circles or ovals. Varying degrees of sophistication can be added to these plots. An important addition is to ensure that the area of the circles reflects the relative size of each of the market segments. Some organizations will then use each circle as a pie chart to identify the proportion of the potential market which they already have. This is useful as it helps to identify where most extra opportunity lies. If an organization already has 95% of a segment's business already, then it may be that extra activity may not be particularly rewarding in this segment.

The DPM is a powerful strategic marketing tool. Why? Well, consider the information required to complete the plots: it is clear that this is the very information any effective marketer would need to know about his or her market. First, to be able to make the y-axis plot the library manager needs to know:

- how the library market breaks down into market segments
- what makes a segment attractive to the library
- what current policies are within the library service
- how each segment scores in the key factors.

Second, to be able to plot the x-axis the library manager needs to know:

- the competitors the library has in each segment served
- what really matters to each user or non-user segment
- how the library offer looks relative to competitor offers for each of these value drivers.

These are real strategic marketing issues. Together these ensure that the most appropriate market audit data is collected (see Chapter 3), not just that which is immediately available. As noted earlier, the library manager may need to estimate in areas where no data exists. Good managers work on sound data whenever they can, but are not afraid to estimate when decisions need to be taken. Waiting for the perfect data can result in what is called 'analysis paralysis', a condition that leads to total inaction while decision makers analyse and re-analyse data in different ways.

Now the segments are plotted, priorities for your marketing strategy can be identified. Within the context of the library's quantified and qualitative ambition it is possible to define an attitude towards each segment, identifying what each might contribute to achieving library ambition, and changes to the offer that will need to be made to ensure that marketing effort is productive. By adding up the expected return from each choice you should reach a figure that goes a long way towards at least meeting the short- to medium-term marketing objectives associated with the ambition. Table 5.4 (overleaf) summarizes possible outcomes from analysing the fictional segments used for the DPM example above (Figure 5.4, page 91).

As can be seen from Table 5.4, when key priorities have been identified the offers made to various groups of users and non-users may either need to be changed (see the next chapter, on marketing strategy and the marketing mix) or may be strong enough already to enable the creation of a good quality informational or reminding campaign with a good chance of early success (see Chapter 7).

Table 5.4   Example outcomes from our fictional DPM example

Segment	DPM position now	DPM position at end of planning period (3 years?)	Offer changes required	Investment costs	Expected return in planning period
Silver Surfers	Relatively attractive, and good offer out there	As now	Maintain current offer, with continuous improvement	Current levels	+10% visits
Cool Kids	Very attractive, but offer is not good at present	Improve offer, to at least parity with competitors	Changes to products and services	+30%, if new funding can be found	+200% visits; +5% issues
Middle Grounders	Very good offer out there, but relatively unattractive	As now, maintain quality of offer but no large investment	No changes required, but remind and inform	Current levels (save 10% on marketing costs)	+5% on issues
Scholars	Relatively unattractive, and not the best offer	As now	No changes required	Current levels	−5% issues; −10% visits

Reflecting upon setting marketing priorities:

- Have you identified a set of priorities for marketing activity?
- Have you undertaken a detailed SWOT analysis by user segment, as well as one for the service as a whole?
- Have you prioritized opportunities and threats by user segment?

Chapter 6

Clear objectives and winning strategies

By the end of this chapter you will have identified objectives by segment and service-wide. You will also have considered the development of marketing strategies and offers for internal stakeholders, external users and non users. The chapter highlights traditional marketing-mix approaches – an expanded four-P to six-P model – and more modern relationship-marketing approaches to strategy.

Having segmented the market (Chapter 4) and decided on priority segments (Chapter 5) and their contribution towards the meeting of quantified marketing objectives and ambition (Chapter 2), it is now time to create marketing strategies to achieve those objectives.

Marketing objectives

Objectives are the 'what' we want to achieve, and strategies are the 'how' we will achieve those objectives. Marketing objectives, like all other objectives, should be SMART – specific, measurable, achievable, realistic and time-specific. Given that they are measurable, marketing objectives in public libraries will relate to items such as issues, visits, enquiries, income generation, website hits or similar. If the objective is to increase awareness or develop the brand, this should be accompanied by pre- and post-campaign measurement. A vague 'objective' to increase awareness is not a good basis for a marketing strategy.

By studying the picture of our options clearly drawn on the DPM (Chapter 5) it is possible to make decisions on priority actions. In other words, when we look at the relative attractiveness of our segments (y-axis of the DPM) in the context of the strength of our offer to each of those segments (x-axis), then it is possible to identify where our efforts are most likely to have impact and where our efforts are likely to fall by the wayside. In addition we should be able to make some estimate of the amount of return possible from each of these segments. Later in this chapter we will discuss the strategies for achieving that return, but at this point it is sufficient to identify some forecast returns for effort. In reality as we consider budget and strategy these objectives will go through a number of iterations until an objective is agreed.

Objectives can either be at service-wide level or segment level. It is best to have both. Remember that objectives are not scientific but are a desired state. Consider your objectives for the planning period. The template shown in Figure 6.1 can be used either for service-wide objectives or objectives by segment (each cell should have a quantified objective; T = current year). If by segment, then you will need one chart for each segment. A series of linked spreadsheets can aggregate a service-wide total.

	T	T+1	T+2	T+3
Issues				
Visits				
Enquiries				
Website hits				
Other				

Figure 6.1   Objectives by segment or service-wide

Such a simple statement of objectives provides context for strategy development. Which strategies will be strong enough to deliver the required level of activity from each segment and in total?

Marketing strategies

A strategy involves undertaking a programme of action to reach a future desired state: taking a public library service from the present to its vision of the future. A useful first stage in this strategy-setting process is to conduct a from–to analysis. In this the senior management team should identify key dimensions of the current position which need to change to a desired future position. Having identified the journey to be taken during the planning period or beyond, the team should then clearly articulate what will be necessary to ensure a successful journey and the issues or risks that arise as a result of the journey. The final column in Figure 6.2 should include initial thoughts on mitigation of risks and problems.

For example, one library strategy may be to go from being a 'bricks and mortar' (e.g. branch library) based service to a more 'clicks and mortar' service (i.e. have an appropriate balance of virtual and physical library based services). The changes required may include investment in IT, new ways of working, and a deeper segmentation of users and non-users to create the appropriate balance. Key issues and risks might include insecure capital expenditure funds, staff resistance to change, and a lack of marketing planning skills to develop the required user understanding. These might be mitigated by investigating several sources of funding, change-management programmes, and staff training in marketing planning tools and techniques.

From	To	Changes required	Key issues or risks that arise and mitigation

Figure 6.2   Template for a from–to analysis

Strategies for internal marketing to stakeholders

Once you are clear about your top-level service-wide strategies, you can look at the marketing strategies which support them. It should be recognized that marketing strategies will need to be formulated for all stakeholder groups, not just users and non-users of the library. You may need to modify your initial thoughts in the light of what is acceptable to these stakeholders. However, even when a modified strategy is agreed, successful communication and implementation will require that stakeholders are managed throughout the planning period.

Stakeholders are those groups or key individuals who are affected by, have a relationship with or have an interest in your library and its marketing planning process. This will include the end-users (or non-users) of your service, but will also include wider groups such as the library committee or trustees, employees, organizations which provide funding for specific initiatives and the media. What interest does each of these (and other) stakeholders have in your marketing strategy? Are they likely to be a positive or negative influence when it comes to implementing that strategy? How can each of the stakeholders be managed to ensure the plan is successfully implemented?

Relationships to manage include those with stakeholders in various categories:

- users: here we have relationships to develop and manage with existing users, new users and lapsed users
- staff: the relationship between senior management and front-line staff will affect the service level provided, and thus an internal marketing strategy is important
- suppliers and partners: including booksellers, publishers, government initiatives, local organizations and groups; in public library terms these include satisfied users, the media, teachers, parents and others.

Bear in mind that some stakeholders can be very influential in encouraging others to use the library. Schools and business organizations are examples in this category. Referral markets are those groups or individuals that can act as advocates for your service. The marketing plan should include ways in which to develop advocacy and viral marketing through such groups or individuals.

Having identified your key stakeholders, complete the template shown in Figure 6.3. It is likely that when you reflect on the interest, power and influences of your stakeholders there is potential for significant conflict. This can be direct conflict with the plan or, and this is more difficult to manage, conflict among the stakeholders themselves. Your strategy may be one of simple communication. Perhaps particular stakeholders need little more than to be kept informed; others may need reminding of where we are in the plan and how it benefits them. In addition, some may need persuading all through the process that real benefits are being achieved by the marketing strategy implementation. As well as a chosen strategy to communicate with them – inform, remind or persuade – your stakeholder strategy may include details of when they should be involved with your implementation, and when they should not be involved. Remember that when you create your marketing action plan later in the process (Chapter 8) you should have appropriate actions to integrate and implement your stakeholder strategy with that for users and non-users.

Key stakeholder	Stakeholder's interest in the marketing strategy	Stakeholder's influence on the implementation of marketing strategy: positive or negative?	Strategy to manage the stakeholder

Figure 6.3   Stakeholder analysis

It is difficult to undertake strategic marketing planning for the public library if the local authority is unaware of the whole range of activities and initiatives supported by the library. Never assume that local government members have any real idea of what the public library does. Even if you have sent every new member of the council an information pack, still do not assume that they fully understand all the issues facing, and the value created by, the public library. Some will have very traditional views about library service and will not be aware of how the library's role is changing. You need to have a section of your marketing plan which has an ongoing annual campaign to keep the library front of mind with such decision makers. If such people are not fully on board then acquiring funds to deliver excellent services to users is relatively difficult. The strategy is to build up a relationship with such people over time so that during a crisis there is an open, friendly, informed relationship, with no misunderstandings.

Marketing strategies for users and non-users

With an understanding of how we can manage our stakeholders it is possible to devise effective marketing strategies to deliver our ambition and objectives. Without such an understanding any marketing strategies are open to risk because they do not take into account one important factor – it is people that make marketing plans succeed or fail. Process is important, but when unforeseen circumstances occur process can be rigid and derail the plan.

Returning to our example of ambition in Chapter 2, where three notional scenarios were offered for a planning period, we can look in more detail at the concepts of marketing objectives and strategy:

- scenario 1: maintain visit levels at 200,000
- scenario 2: increase visit levels to 300,000
- scenario 3: Increase visit levels to 500,000.

Top-level quantified objectives and ambition focus the mind well when considering our marketing-specific objectives. Marketing objectives will be individual quantified targets by segment, or, in business language, products or services sold into markets. Together this set of marketing objectives should add up to the quantified total ambition. If we cannot create a set of realistic (even if challenging) marketing objectives that add up to this ambition, then we really have been overconfident in the early stages of planning. 'Stretch' goals can be invigorating but objectives which clearly cannot be met do nothing but demotivate staff.

Marketing objectives, as noted above, are about products or services to specific markets. To ensure that we employ appropriate strategies to generate the level of return we plan for, then it is useful to consider a well-established strategic marketing tool, the Ansoff matrix and adapt it for public libraries.

Given that marketing objectives are about products and services sold into specific types of market, this matrix reveals the four key strategy options we have for the delivery of such objectives in the public library context (see Figure 6.4). We shall now look at each of these four options in detail.

| | | 'Offer' (Products/services) | |
		Existing	New
Community group or segment	Existing	Increase use of existing 'offer' by existing group(s) (market penetration)	Make a new 'offer' to existing group(s) (new product development)
	New	Find new group(s) of users to use existing 'offer' (market extension)	Set up a new 'offer' for a group that doesn't currently use the library (diversification)

Figure 6.4   Service development options
(Adapted from the Ansoff Matrix)

1   *Generating more activity from existing user segments by communicating and promoting our existing products and services – a market penetration strategy.* In many instances this is the least risky of the four options. We are likely to have a good understanding of this group of users and also the current range of products and services we offer. Other people in this segment who do not currently use us are likely to respond to our offer, as we have a good understanding of their needs and a history of success with the products and services we have offered to

people like them. As part of this strategy we might cross-sell or up-sell (cross-selling attempts to encourage customers to buy related products, while up-selling encourages them to buy more high value products). Such a strategy might be, for instance, to inform or remind users of other formats for the subjects they are interested in. A keen reader of fiction might be made aware of the opportunities for hearing fiction in the car through CD books; a borrower of DVDs on exercise workouts might be told about the whole range of books available on healthy living. This sort of strategy will, to be effective, use the data and permissions from reader transactions.

2   *Generating more activity from communicating and promoting our existing products and services to new segments who currently do not use the library – a market extension strategy.* In effect, we are using our existing products and services to extend the market without the need to develop any new offerings. This strategy is appropriate where we believe that there are segments out there which do not currently use the library in any great numbers but who, if they only knew about it and the benefits it offers them personally, would become users. In other words we have the right offer but non-users just don't know about it. This market extension strategy has the advantage that we understand our products and services well and are able to deliver them in full and consistently. However, our knowledge of this type of user group is limited as we have not had a close relationship with it. The risk to this strategy is that we do not understand the user segment enough, and mistakenly believe our standard offer is likely to be a winner with them. As we have noted, one size does not fit all. For success in this type of strategy we must be aware of the important, perhaps small, differences between our existing users and user groups which do not currently take up our offer. Slight alteration or customization may be the difference between success or failure in this strategy.

3   *Generating more activity from developing new products and services for existing user segments.* In instances where we believe that existing user segments are important to our future but are currently using our services as much as we could reasonably expect, a new product development strategy is appropriate. In such a strategy we should use

our close understanding of the needs, lifestyles and other segmentation variables of these user groups to look for innovative and attractive new service delivery or contents. Sometimes this will be an entirely new type of material on offer, while on other occasions the strategy may be to find new ways to distribute library services, perhaps from afar.

4   *Generating new activity from developing new products and services for new user segments.* This diversification strategy is the most risky of all but has the potential to transform an organization. However, in the current business world, diversification is not perceived to be an attractive strategy. This is because diversification takes an organization into new customer areas where the needs and wants of those customers are not well enough understood to allow the organization to confidently predict the response to its offers. This understanding cannot be achieved simply by surveying these new groups and responding to what they say they want. Furthermore, the new products and services developed may, at best, be stretching the competencies and capabilities of the organization and, at worst, taking it into areas where it is unlikely to deliver its offer. Although this is the most risky marketing strategy it is often the one that public libraries are instructed to address or choose to follow.

Having identified our four strategy options for generating the activity levels we require to meet our objectives, we now need to identify where these objectives are coming from and what the relative mix of strategies will be. Will all new activity come from new users? Or 50% from new users and 50% from existing users? Or 75% from existing users? It is instructive to look at your ambition and divide this into marketing objectives by the options offered by the Ansoff matrix. It can be revealing to simply take the four boxes and allocate 100% between the options and physically write this into the matrix. Such an activity will force you to keep objectives and strategies closely aligned. Once you are clear on the relative proportion of new activity to be generated by each of these four strategies, the choice of marketing communications and promotions become relatively easier than if you did not have this background.

For instance, if you identified 'Cool Kids' as a priority segment in Chapter 5, then you may consider developing this as a market extension strategy (there are existing products and services which, if communicated well, will attract) or diversification strategy (you need to create new products and services to attract and interest this new user segment). If you also have a marketing objective that Cool Kids will account for, say, an extra 20,000 visits next year, then you have a good information base upon which to develop very detailed strategies within this broad strategy. What would you have to do not only to make them aware you exist, but to be reasonably confident that a footfall of 20,000 would be reasonable during the given period?

Creating the 'offers' for users and non-users

In practice there are a number of strategies which public libraries have to define. These include service strategies, site strategies and other management strategies (e.g. staff). There may be a call for user and non-user strategies (marketing would define these as customer retention and customer acquisition strategies) and marketing will add segmentation and one-to-one strategies. One-to-one strategies are highly customized library offers.

There are likely to be three elements to an effective marketing strategy for public libraries:

- general service-wide marketing strategies
- specific segment marketing strategies
- customer relationship management strategies.

General service-wide marketing strategies will be about creating a basic marketing infrastructure which is strong enough to support a series of segment-specific offers. This level will include the management of brand and sub-brands, ensuring that the brand is neither too general to be of little interest to anyone in particular, nor too specific to potentially distance or exclude key user segments.

Segment-specific strategies will configure an offer around the value proposition developed for each segment. Customer relationship management strategies will take these segment offers and personalize them for individual users.

With the broad library strategy in place you now need to move on to very detailed strategies for individual segments (both existing and new) which can be supported by a tactical one-year marketing plan. This strategy development includes the creation of 'offers' based upon the elements of the marketing mix. 'Offers' here does not mean a promotional offer such as a free video loan but rather it means the general combination of elements which the library believes will be the physical manifestation of the value proposition for the segment.

Traditionally marketing 'offers' have been developed around a marketing mix of elements within the four Ps – product, price, place, promotion. Others have turned these around and described them from the customer's point of view as the four Cs – customer needs, cost, convenience, communication. Consultancies and academics have added other Ps over the years – some of the most common are packaging, people and physical evidence. Libraries might like to consider politics and partnerships as extra Ps, making a six-P model, as these are often encouraged and are necessary for financial reasons, as well as because of political concerns, in some library authorities. There are, of course, other Ps which could be added, such as perceptions and packaging.

In recent years there has been some dissatisfaction with the traditional four-P marketing mix model, and the emphasis has shifted to relationship marketing – in other words, being driven by developing one-to-one relationships with individual customers rather than mass marketing to a general customer base. To reflect this, our strategy and 'offer' should include a statement of the type of relationship we want with the segment. Some segments will not benefit from a close relationship (perhaps because they themselves do not naturally feel the need to have a close relationship), while others segments may prefer to have a close relationship with the library.

Whether the library service articulates strategy at a very general level or, preferably, at a detailed segment or even one-to-one (CRM, see p. 121) level, it will need to consider its offers in terms of the six-P marketing mix (product, price, place, promotion, politics, partnerships) noted above. We shall look at each of these elements in detail.

Product (customer needs).

In essence, what products and services should be provided as part of the modern library service, and how should this offer be made to users and non-users? It is perhaps instructive to think of a 'pizza of products and services' which should be made available if all legitimate users' and non-users' needs and wants can be met. Our general strategy would be to make sure that we have all of this in place, and the segment-specific strategy would be, for marketing purposes, to reconfigure the pizza slices into dishes for the specific segments. This will usually mean strongly marketing only part of the service to each user segment, while perhaps gently informing them of the wider range of materials on offer.

In Figure 6.5 the circle represents the set of products and services which covers all the requirements of the set of value propositions for the segments we serve. The general marketing strategy is to keep this infrastructure in place. The more powerful marketing strategies, however, will be those by segments which sell hard on the key elements of service required by them. For instance segment 3 is particularly interested in only two slices of the library pizza. While there is always the potential to cross-sell into other slices, the most powerful marketing will be to provide an offer based on these two slices which we can then communicate with a strong message. A notable exception would be where this segment is already making full use of the two parts of the service which fit the value proposition for the segment and is unlikely to be stimulated into extra use,

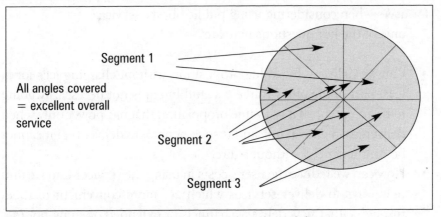

Figure 6.5 Get the products and service pizza right

regardless of the persuasiveness of our marketing message. In such instances cross-selling to other slices might be a potential strategy but almost certainly not a highly successful one, unless the segment genuinely wants and needs the benefits of other parts of the service. And if that were the case we should have identified that during the research phase for the creation of the value proposition.

Marketing all products and services to everyone will always have the potential to return some response from those who are naturally able to quickly understand for themselves what library service may mean to them. We should not assume that this can be generalized across the whole population. There is a need to make it clear to particular segments just what library services mean to them. To complicate the offer with marketing communications about products and services which do not particularly interest them is likely to deflect rather than attract their attention. Less can be more – consider the way that many retailers have created space rather than fill their showrooms with more and more products. The products we offer should gain attention not create 'noise'.

Price (cost)

Even where there is a strong commitment to free service with no charge or fee for any aspect of the service, it would be foolish to think that, from the user's point of view, there are no costs involved. As noted earlier there may be transport costs, time and energy costs (including dealing with the bureaucracy of many library processes), or other opportunity costs for users when considering using public library services.

Some of the key questions here are:

- Can we deliver a full value proposition without charging fees for at least part of the offer? A free part-fulfilment is not necessarily going to be acceptable if it is a value proposition that has power only when delivered on time in full, and is so expensive to deliver that it cannot be countenanced without a direct fee.
- How can we reduce the user's costs in using the service? Can we find new ways to deliver services which are more convenient to them through either new delivery channels or extended opening hours?

- Are we aware of the relative costs and value to the user of using the competition, such as bookshops and video rental outlets?

Place (convenience)

The 'place' element of the marketing mix is all about the channels or 'routes to market' we need to employ to deliver efficient and effective service to users. It is most obviously seen in the number and location of our branches and mobile libraries, but modern approaches will consider 'place' not simply a physical place but a more abstract place – any way of delivering service: static or remote.

As with product we will have a set of routes to market which will enable us to offer, from the user's viewpoint, convenient access to the product and services we offer. Certain segments may need to have particular routes to market stressed. For example, business people away from home for several nights every week may prefer to access services remotely from their hotels, rather than through static service points when they return.

Promotion and advocacy (communication)

Promotion and advocacy can be a mix of advertising, sales promotions, public relations and attendance at events, or visiting specific client groups to discuss the library and its services. Some segments will require a strategy which does little more than inform or remind. Other segments will require a persuasive promotional strategy which will include inducements to try the library service. Non-users are unlikely to be 'bribed' into the library – do not expect free offers (e.g. free DVD loans as inducements) to be successful unless the overall offer is right. A good principle to follow is that 'free stuff' should be offered as a reward to existing library users to encourage more library use. Non-users require a stronger offer than 'free'.

Advocacy, or making the case for the public library, can be encouraged by creating a database of materials which can be used to support the public library. Such materials are often held on websites. For example, in the USA, www.oclc.org/advocacy/default.htm; in the UK, www.eemlac.co.uk/info/advocacy/index.jsp; and in Australia, http://alia.org.au/advocacy/.

Advocacy can include making a case for the library contribution to local economic or social capital: see www.libsci.sc.edu/SCEIS/home.htm (South Carolina) and http://dlis.dos.state.fl.us/bld/roi/publications.cfm (Florida). You may even find support from agencies which are not public libraries. For instance, in the UK the Reading Agency www.readingagency.org.uk has a range of advocacy materials, as does the National Literacy Trust, www.theliteracytrust.org.uk; www.schoollibrariesadvocacy.org.uk has a toolkit. As noted earlier, quotable quotes are very useful for marketing, and the Canadian Library Association has some interesting examples of the type of quotes you might use (www.cla.ca/divisions/capl/advocacy/quotes.htm). Chapter 7 will consider in more depth the marketing communications requirements for an effective promotional strategy.

Politics

By their very nature libraries are public sector organizations subject to the democratic political process. As such they are likely to have changing political masters, and must create and communicate marketing messages to each of the range of stakeholders. Libraries support all shades of political and social activity and should have no difficulty in creating this set of messages where individual messages change in their emphasis as the democratic process unfolds.

Partnerships

Libraries have always sought close relationships with organizations with whom they share a similar or complementary mission or objective. St Louis Public Library (US), for instance, views every community agency, business or institution as a potential partner for either funding, time or benefits in kind. In return the partner receives publicity, and library users become aware of its services. This is an excellent basis for marketing, as such partnerships rarely incur significant direct costs and provide great opportunity for referral. Referral is one of the most powerful marketing activities that can be stimulated.

Libraries can no longer stay isolated as a minor part of local government, for they may find that the world will simply pass them by. It is unlikely that large sums of investment money are likely to be directed solely at libraries in the near future, which suggests that joint bids for funds with partners is an appropriate marketing strategy. Additionally, partners can sometimes add weight to the library offer for particular segments.

A partnership strategy can be an important contribution to the delivery of the marketing plan. Partnerships can be with other public sector organizations or be with private sector organizations. Public sector partnerships are more likely to benefit from a shared culture, while private sector partnerships will introduce new thinking.

Beware of partnerships for the 'general good' which are time-consuming without showing quick benefits. Partnerships benefit from having specific goals whether as a learning alliance or as a service alliance. They can support your marketing strategy and plan as partners in funding, research, building audiences, developing and delivering services, and training. Inevitably they can be difficult to manage with issues of power and trust.

Relationship marketing as a strategy

In recent years the traditional marketing mix model of marketing has been criticized as being too mechanistic and based upon organizations trying to get customers to see it their way rather than in developing products, services and offers according to the customer's requirements. This approach has often resulted in very impersonal isolated marketing messages which have been easy to ignore or have irritated as much as they have inspired.

Modern marketing recognizes that creating business relationships with customers is likely to be more effective than simple mass marketing. Customer relationship management (CRM) is a structured way to think about developing and managing such relationships. CRM should not be thought of simply in terms of customer service or user satisfaction. In a public library context CRM is a strategy based upon the sustained and focused use of user information, to attract and keep users through ongoing conversations which build long-lasting, mutually beneficial relationships. All elements of this definition are important, but emphasis should be on the final clause – mutually beneficial relationships. CRM is founded on both the user and the library service achieving measurable benefits. Given the political importance of developing partnerships with other organizations, public libraries are natural users of relationship marketing techniques.

Note also that CRM is a series of tools and techniques rather than simply technology. With CRM it is easy to buy the technology from vendors without achieving the benefits which the approach can bring. Before you embark on a CRM project be absolutely sure what you expect it to deliver and be clear on how that can and will be delivered (if you have undertaken the work suggested in Chapters 3 and 4 you will be off to a sound start). Then and only then look for IT vendors who can provide what you need. 'Off the shelf' packages should be treated with caution.

Many CRM applications in business are simply attempts to get back to the corner-shop mentality where the shopkeeper knew every customer and was able to tailor service to their individual needs and highlight new products to buy which were highly relevant. As companies and organizations grew bigger this level of customer understanding reduced and a more distant relationship with customers became common. Modern approaches look to create this customer intimacy again. Public libraries have traditionally been very good at maintaining relationships with users at branch library level. The tradition of keeping books under the counter for regular readers is one example of this relationship. However, recent initiatives to attract new user groups that the library has little existing understanding of, or relationship with, have highlighted the importance of relationship management with the consequent need to investigate CRM strategies and techniques as part of a marketing planning process.

As we have already noted, not all readers are the same. CRM offers the potential to personalize service on the basis of a deep understanding of the user. In terms of existing users this may mean a regular e-mail update, based on past borrowing habits or expressed preferences, of new additions to the library. For non-users CRM will emphasize customer service and offer development.

Whether such personalization is worthwhile will depend upon a number of factors.

1   *Diversity of user needs.* Where user needs are very similar among individuals within a segment, personalization of the overall offer will

not deliver great benefits for either the individual or the library service. However, where even within a segment there are still significant differences, then there are significant benefits in personalizing the service within the segment. For instance, disability will suggest personalization of the service to reflect the unique needs of each person.

2 *Distribution of lifetime values.* The concept of lifetime value views the user or non-user as having a potential level of usage within their lifetime as a user of that service. For example, in many market segments people move home every five to seven years, sometimes within the library authority area and sometimes outside it. If we could expect two visits a month and six book issues from each of these users then clearly over their lifetime as a user they can, individually, be very important contributors to our ability to meet our performance targets. It might be worth personalizing and customizing the service for these users to encourage loyalty and repeat visits and uses.

On the other hand, individual tourists may only visit the area once or twice in their lifetime. In such cases the offer should be a first class general offer to tourists (based around segment needs rather than detailed individual needs) with customization and personalization undertaken only where there is a clear return on investment.

If all members of a particular segment have similar visits, issues, enquiry or political potential for the library service, then this will be a factor to take into account when considering service personalization. Clearly if potential is the same across the segment then extra effort may not bring extra return. Similarly, if one segment has a significantly higher potential return than another, then personalization may be an option to consider.

3 *Ease of tailoring the offer and interactions.* Inevitably there are significant barriers to tailoring library services. Tailored services can be complex and expensive, and it can be difficult to manage expectations. If these barriers are high then the benefits from any tailoring may be low.

A final thought to consider when assessing the potential for personalization is: 'Should the offer, the message or both be personalized?' It is perfectly reasonable to personalize the message but not the offer, if appropriate.

To undertake effective CRM as part of your marketing plan you need:

1 *A database of user contacts and activity.* Personalizing the offer, message or service relationship can be undertaken only in the context of an excellent information base on users and non-users.
2 *Analyses of the database.* The database is of no practical use unless tools exist to analyse the information and look for meaningful patterns which can influence offer development, marketing communications or service delivery.
3 *To build relationships with targeted users.* CRM requires relationships with existing users. Without developing such relationships CRM is unlikely to have any purpose, impact or outcome.
4 *Privacy policies.* CRM is a very data-intensive approach to developing service. Users are unlikely to allow you to collect data about them unless they are convinced that it is safe with you. Trust is key.
   As yourself, 'Why should users give the library their data?' Remember that your CRM activity should be based on permission marketing – marketing which the user or non-user specifically requests and accepts. It is significantly better to have 'opt in' communications rather than 'opt out'. 'Opt in' means that users specifically agree to receive marketing messages and communications from you. 'Opt out' means that the library claims the right to send users marketing materials unless they specifically tell you not to. In some countries legislation will mean that opt-in is the only legal approach to CRM. Even where 'opt out' is allowed, it is still more acceptable to establish an 'opt in' policy.
5 *Metrics.* CRM is about creating mutually beneficial relationships, so it is important to monitor whether these benefits do accrue as expected. In addition to the normal activity-based issues and visits, it is important, in the CRM approach, to measure the implementation of user strategy (e.g. cost to serve, satisfaction levels), operational strategy (e.g. response levels, complaints) and infrastructure (e.g. call answering times, response times to enquiries).

Finalizing the offer for specific segments

Now that you have considered the marketing mix model (via a six-P approach) and the issues behind relationship marketing, it is time to create an offer for each segment of the market identified in Chapter 4. Although you may have a general offer for a number of segments, it is very important to have a distinct offer for each of the priority segments identified in Chapter 5. There are certain segments where you want not just a good offer but the winning offer, as support and activity from these segments is very important to the future health of the library service. The differences between the defined offers for individual segments will have important implications for marketing communications (Chapter 7).

Bringing together this understanding of segmentation, the value proposition for each segment, and the marketing and relationship mix for each segment, you can now create an offer for each segment. In reality, good marketing will build the service around a key marketing mix infrastructure and use relationship marketing tools and techniques to customize. The key decision is how to create a balance of marketing mix and relationship strategies to meet the quantified marketing objectives.

Complete the template shown in Figure 6.6 (overleaf) to ensure that as part of your marketing strategy each of your segments has a genuinely interesting, and hopefully compelling, offer based on the value proposition for each segment derived in Chapter 4. This chart will provide an important input into the marketing communications decisions to be made in Chapter 7. Marketing communications to specific segments are not just about slogans, but will address messages about the product or service, its costs (both direct and indirect), the way it can be delivered and any promotional campaign associated with it. The degree of relationship you have with the segment already or wish to have will be important in determining the tone of the campaign. Other stakeholders (hence the political and partners rows) will, in best practice, be part of the marketing campaign.

Some other aspects of marketing strategy for public libraries

Before moving on to marketing communications in Chapter 7, there are several other areas of interest to the marketing strategy practitioner in public libraries. While developing strategy it is important to remain aware of the user life cycle, the need to build loyalty within the user base, branding,

	Segment A	Segment B	Segment C
Product or service			
Price, or costs reduced for user/non-user			
Key ways to access the product or service (place)			
Promotional activity			
Politics			
Partners in the offer and their contribution			
Relationships strategy (How close to the segment are we? How close do we want to be?)			

Figure 6.6   The library offer to specific segments

managing users' experience of the service when they come to use it, and ensuring that we satisfy them and at least meet their reasonable expectations. In other words, it is important as part of our strategy to make sure that we will be able to deliver the offers and promises we have created.

Managing the user life cycle

An important dimension of marketing and CRM is the recognition that there is a life cycle to the user's relationship with the library service. This means that there are certain important 'touch points' that need to be managed in different ways to recognize the depth of the relationship at that point in its development. We all expect this to be recognized in our dealings with services, both public and private. How often have you been annoyed when an organization you buy from always requests your full details every time you make contact with them?

In marketing management a life cycle can be applied to customers, products or brand. It has a number of stages: introduction, growth, maturity, decline and collapse. Adapting the concept we can characterize the library user life cycle, as in Figure 6.7.

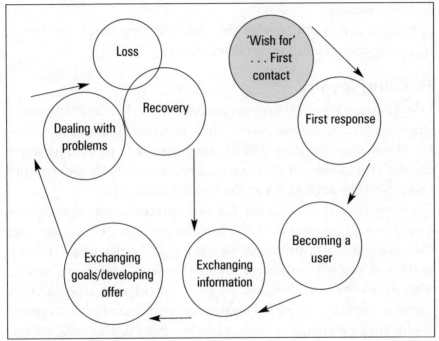

Figure 6.7   User life cycle

The life cycle begins with an unawareness of the library service when the non-user will be identified and receive communications from the library. For whatever reason she or he may, after this first contact, make a first response which may be to call the library or visit to see if what is offered truly is there in support of the communication. If this experience is positive, then the person will become a user and by the very fact of borrowing materials or using the computers will be potentially exchanging information with the library service about that use. After a number of successful contacts with the library the user is likely to feel some degree of relationship with the library and its staff, and will be willing to feed back important information which can help the library develop its offer to both existing users and potential new users. In addition, the library will have the potential to build up a database of past interactions with the user (e.g. issues) which can be used to tailor the offer in the future. Some of these users will feel able to share their own personal goals, which the astute librarian will be able to include in thinking around service development and customization.

Further discussion of what this user life cycle means for library marketing communications is offered on pages 156–8.

Building loyalty

One of the most important elements of a marketing and customer relationship strategy is to recognize that once you have managed to attract a user to use the library, then the most difficult thing may be to get that person to become a regular user, or even come in for a second time! Some marketing effort should be directed at a loyalty building strategy.

Loyalty is a difficult concept. For some private sector organizations, loyalty means little more than simple repeat purchases. Others, however, particularly service organizations such as public libraries, would do better to think of loyalty as an attitude towards the service provider. Consider what people feel loyal towards: families, sports teams, schools, clubs, cultures, countries. People feel loyal to communities rather than organizations. Their experience of using public libraries will determine whether they feel part of the library community or are simply interacting with just another organization. Loyalty can only be won if you deliver your promise well, sort out problems fast and show a genuine commitment to help the user get to where he or she is going in their lives, whether their goal is simply a good read or a valued place in society. In addition, loyalty can be encouraged by having a mission or vision that users really associate with and would support as a 'good thing'.

Branding

Many public libraries have sought to change the image of the service by rebranding, sometimes as in the case of Tower Hamlets in the UK, moving significantly from the vocabulary of the library to a more modern terminology, as Idea Store.

Rebranding the library is not to be undertaken lightly. There are strong traditional values in the idea of the public library which many commercial organizations would be very proud to have in their marketing kitbag. To move away from this may, in an attempt to instil new values into the idea of a library, damage the well-proven existing values. However, the world is constantly changing, so it is not an option to stand still risking an archaic position in the public's mindset.

Any strategy to rebrand should be considered carefully. Remember that when companies rebrand they often allocate very significant amounts of money for such exercises and realize that there may well be a need to revisit this in five to ten years. On other occasions their product or service is so right for the times and delivers as promised that viral marketing builds the brand. Google, for example, is not known as a large spender on advertising. Word of mouth has been extremely important. Public libraries do not have the financial resources to ride the waves of branding and rebranding. Do they have a powerful product which will encourage word of mouth?

If you do decide on a rebrand as part of your strategy, ensure you employ professional help. Branding is not something the senior management team can do around the table. Also remember that the messages you decide to put out as part of your branding exercise may or may not ring true with users and non-users. Brand is derived from what others think about you, not from what you decide is the way you wish to be perceived. Any branding exercise will need to affect the whole culture of the organization to ensure the experience matches the promise.

User experience management

Having looked at the value of library services to users on their terms (segmentation), created and communicated offers around this and recognized the marketing implications of the user life cycle, we need to manage the user's experience of using the service. What do we want the user to feel, sense, think and do when they are using the library (see Figure 6.8, overleaf)? Are we managing this well? Finally, how do we want the user to relate to us? Is our messaging clear on this so we can manage user expectations well?

	What response do we want from users?	Will they naturally make this response?	If 'yes', how can we enhance the experience? If 'no', how can we make it 'yes'?
Feel			
Sense			
Think			
Do			

Figure 6.8   Managing the user's experience

The user's experience of the library will be based upon their interaction with a number of key dimensions:

- *Communications.* All your communications create an impression, good or bad. Are they professional, setting the right tone?
- *Identity/brand.* Will the user want to be associated with you? Remember there are a number of different library user and non-user segments. We need to manage brand very carefully if we are to maintain all segments as loyal users.
- *People.* Your staff are a marketing asset. It is no good having policy and process in place if the front-line staff present a different experience from that promised by your marketing communications.
- *Systems and processes.* Do things work in practice as promised by your marketing message? Is the user experience consistent with what you believe is the offer? Are the processes visible and understandable by users? Is there an appropriate combination of automation and personal touch? Given that it takes a powerful message to woo users into the library, there should be powerful controls on the process to ensure that when they come into the library they are not disappointed. It is not the first visit to the library that is most difficult to achieve – it is the second.

From a marketer's point of view there is no one perfect process. A marketing-friendly process will allow different approaches within an overarching system. Why? Because, as we noted in Chapter 4, segmentation is key to effective marketing planning, and segmentation will almost always reveal different ways in which your users and non-users wish to access library services. There is no one point in the process where things can go wrong. Things will go wrong at different points in the process for different people. To see how important this can be, consider the process of making a cup of tea. As Figure 6.9 shows, even such a simple process as making a cup of tea can have at least 15 potential steps in it. You may be able to add more.

Simplified process:

1. Find out how the drinkers like their tea
2. Consider the environment in which it will be served
3. Fill the kettle
4. Switch the kettle on
5. Ensure that a clean, dry cup/mug and spoon are available
6. Put milk in cup/mug
7. Warm the teapot
8. Choose brand of tea
9. Put tea/teabags in teapot
10. Pour boiling water into the teapot
11. Allow to brew
12. Pour tea into cup/mug
13. Add sugar to taste
14. Stir
15. Present in most appealing way

Figure 6.9   Making a cup of tea

Where should the marketer look for the weak link in delivering the promise? To look for the weak links from a purely mechanical point of view is useful but not sufficient to support the marketing effort. Remember, different segments will have different views on where things go wrong, and it is better to work from a segment point of view than an abstract view of the best possible process. Working from a cost and economy view is acceptable given the usual economic constraints. However, be careful here because it is not best value to spend less money but reduce issues, visits or enquiries by creating economical processes which just do not allow the service to meet the expectation of users and non-users.

In our example of making a cup of tea, for instance, things can go wrong all through the process. For one segment, not enough or too much milk may have been put in (stage 6). For another, we may choose the wrong brand of tea (stage 8). Presenting the tea in the most appealing way may also prove a stumbling block (stage 15) – some people prefer to drink tea out of fine quality china, while others are happy to drink out of a mug.

Marketing planners will often deconstruct processes to identify weak points in the delivery of offers to specific segments. In library terms consider:

- *The environment.* Is the atmosphere in the library consistent with your marketing messages? If not, worry!
- *Products and services.* Finally, and most basic of all, are you delivering what you promise in your marketing communications? If you are, then the user will feel, sense and think all the things you hoped they would. If not, then not only will the disappointment discourage them but you can be sure that should anyone ask their opinion of the library they will be non-committal at best and negative at worst.

Every time a member of the public comes into contact with your staff and service, a good or a bad impression is created based on their experience of that contact – a 'moment of truth'. Your marketing communications will almost certainly have offered a positive experience in store for those visiting and using the library. What are your 'moments of truth' like? Excellent, okay, or bad? You will be surprised at just how many there are. Jan Carlzon, former President of SAS Airlines (and author of the book *Moments of Truth*), believed his company had 50,000 moments of truth every day. That's 50,000 times a day when either a good or bad impression was made about his airline.

How many moments of truth does your library face every day, and how closely do you manage them? To get a quick impression of how many, do the following calculation:

Number of people who visit you per day

X

number of staff they interact with

This is likely to be a very big number even without factoring in the number of impressions created by people who did not interact with the staff but just received impressions as they walked around the library. Readers will notice staff dress standards and body language. The furniture, equipment, condition of stock, its neatness and tidiness along with the general condition of the building will all make an impression. These are all marketing issues. Are you happy with how you manage these moments of truth?

As a marketer of public library services you should be looking to maximize the number of positive moments (maybe by increasing the amount of positive contacts when they are identified) and fixing the negative contacts, whether these have resulted in a complaint or not. Indeed, the public library service will never be a learning organization until it encourages comments and complaints. Unfortunately in many public libraries there is a marked fear of complaints because of the political impact they can have for politicians.

Having, in your marketing communication, promised an experience of using the library, then you are duty-bound to monitor that experience. Some ways in which you can do this include regular and 'snapshot' research, monitoring satisfaction and encouraging user complaints and compliments.

User satisfaction

The aim of a public library is to satisfy the needs and wants of as many legitimate users as possible while employing resources optimally. Dissatisfied users are more likely to tell friends and colleagues about their experience of the library than satisfied readers are. Hence satisfied customers are an important viral marketing channel, and customer satisfaction is an important marketing strategy.

Despite being a prerequisite for a positive relationship with users, a high satisfaction score does not automatically lead to loyalty or even a repeat visit. Think of your own experience. You may be highly satisfied with a product or service but may, for all sorts of other reasons, not buy that product or service next time when you need that sort of thing. There can be many reasons for this: you may be persuaded away by the marketing of others; other alternatives may have just introduced a new or innovative product which delights you rather than simply satisfies you; you may just want a change! For many years I bought a specific brand of car which I was very happy with. However, recently I changed to another brand partly because it offered something new and partly because I did just fancy a change. Simply monitoring my customer satisfaction scores would not have helped the motor manufacturer to predict my future purchasing intentions confidently.

Marketers know that the relationship between satisfaction and customer retention is weaker the stronger the competitive intensity in the industry. Given that there are an increasing number of competitors providing similar, though not the same, services as the public library, then it is likely that loyalty is a key issue to manage. Some may say that public libraries have more competition but nobody does it in the combination we do. This, while true, is likely to take our eye off the ball. Remember that user segments do not buy the library service as a whole but rather those parts of the 'library pizza' that matter to them. In such circumstances individual competitors need only provide high-quality delivery of the benefits these users seek to tempt them away to try another approach and, if found to be more convenient, retain them as customers. To be 'generally satisfied' is most certainly not an indication of loyalty or future use.

Given the complexity of segmentation and the nature of customer satisfaction, it is important to look for areas where things can go wrong. Assessing user satisfaction is not simply a process of asking users what they think of you, but involves proactively putting yourself in the position of users and honestly evaluating what that experience is like.

Where are the roots of dissatisfaction

Service marketers and academics such as Parasuraman (whose ideas influenced the development of LIBQUAL+ used by a number of academic libraries to track library performance in meeting user expectations - see www.libqual.org) have identified a number of gaps between the view of the providers of products and services and the buyers or users of those products and services. Let us consider this thinking in a public library context in Figure 6.10.

Some potential roots of failure to meet user expectations:

- Politicians' and users' expectations differ
- Management understanding of users' needs and wants is not what they actually want
- The service is configured in a way that is not helpful to users
- The promised service is not delivered by library management
- Partnership arrangements fail, resulting in failed service
- Library management and external partners fail to co-ordinate responsibilities
- Users' expectations are not managed by library management to ensure that users have reasonable rather than unreasonable expectations.

Figure 6.10 Addressing potential failures to meet user expectations of service

If we accept that the immediate concern is to ensure that we meet user expectations and then, wherever possible, exceed them, we need to be clear about how users get their expectations of the library service. Users' expectations relate to their needs and what they think is realistically possible. Hopefully we have managed their expectations through our marketing effort so that they expect a service that, from our side, we believe we can deliver. Users will have received marketing messages from us or from friends and colleagues (in effect, viral marketing for us). Their expectations will have been influenced by their past experience of using the service and they will have a tacit concept of what it is reasonable to expect. Where they have no past experience of using the service there is a danger that they may have unreasonable expectations (either due to overambitious marketing by us or misunderstanding by them) that need to be managed. This management of user expectation is very important and should reflect the complexity of different types of users. Some have very high expectations, perhaps from having previously lived in a neighbouring authority where greater funds were available to support libraries. Others may have very low expectations and thus may not even consider the library as a realistic player in the options to help them meet their needs.

Satisfaction may be measured by the answers to a few key satisfaction questions, a focus group to study 'How are we doing?', monitoring of compliments and complaints or an unobtrusive test, sometimes called mystery shopping (Chapter 3).

Unobtrusive testing is an excellent technique for investigating whether the offer we have developed for our user groups is indeed delivered on time in full in the library. It is one thing to create a policy about how the library will operate, and quite another to deliver that service. What is the user's experience of that delivery – good or bad? Unobtrusive testing, where an anonymous tester turns up without prior notice, can answer that question. It should be noted that such a technique needs to be implemented with sensitivity, as no one likes to be monitored without their knowledge. This should not be used as a technique to test staff but rather a method to identify training needs and changes which need to be made to existing processes if users are to receive the offer in full.

Now that you have a marketing strategy for your plan, an understanding of stakeholder interest and a set of offers for your segments, and have reflected upon the issues around delivering the offer, it is time to formulate and communicate a set of marketing messages and communications (Chapter 7) and ensure than the plan is effectively and efficiently implemented (Chapter 8).

Reflection upon the creation of marketing strategies and offers:

- Are your marketing objectives specific, measurable, achievable, realistic and time-specific (SMART)?
- Have you a clear idea of where your marketing strategies will take you?
- Have you a marketing strategy for internal and other stakeholders as well as users and non-users?
- Does your marketing strategy include differentiated offers for specific segments?
- Do you have a relationship marketing strategy?
- Are you managing the user life cycle, and the user experience, and encouraging loyalty?
- Is your marketing strategy supported by a commitment to developing and monitoring customer satisfaction?

Chapter 7

Attention-grabbing marketing communications

In this chapter you will find ideas on how to market your offers to your market segments through traditional and modern marketing communications approaches. You will also find principles of effective promotion and a brief discussion of websites as a marketing communication.

Having defined our ambition (Chapter 2), studied the market for public library services in our authority (Chapter 3), segmented the user and non-user base and created value propositions for each (Chapter 4), looked at the strategic priorities for activity according to an understanding of what each segment can contribute towards meeting our performance measures during the planning period (Chapter 5), and devised marketing objectives and strategies for the planning period (Chapter 6), we can now move to the area which is often the first thought of a public librarian when thinking of marketing – communication and promotions.

Successful communications

Remember that there are five basic elements to successful communications: the communicator sending the message; the message itself; the medium used to convey the message; the intended recipient of the message; and feedback to ensure the message has been received and has been understood in the way it was intended. This is an important process to manage, and is not simply a case of the public librarian devising publicity materials, distributing them in the most economical way possible and then standing back to receive the expected rush of new recruits to the library.

If we have undertaken all of the previous work in this book well, then the messages we wish to broadcast will be clear and well targeted. Although there will be some general awareness-building messages and supporting advertising and publicity materials it is likely that the more powerful messages will be based on offers to specific segments, offers which will help these people move forward in their journey to wherever they wish to go in their lives. When we have devised the right message some thought must be given to how it should be conveyed (on paper or in person, for instance) and how we will be sure that the message has been received and understood.

National government bodies and professional associations often set the scene for individual public library authorities to build upon. In England the MLA has undertaken work on branding and a national marketing strategy and plan. In the US more than 20,000 academic, school, public and special libraries across the country are participating in the American Library Association's Campaign for America's Libraries. This successful campaign is supported by a wealth of advertising materials and other resources and will now run until 2010.

All library authorities should take advantage of national work where possible and build on it in their localities. With regard to the need to drive planning by segments, it is highly likely that most authorities will develop other supplementary materials to reflect their own priorities and user segments.

Addressing users, non-users and stakeholders

Remember also that your marketing communications are not just addressed to users and non-users: as part of implementing a wide marketing strategy for the development of your public library services you also have to have communications with other stakeholders such as council members and staff. These 'internal markets' provide the sound basis for delivering effective services direct to users. Marketing communications activities to these people will include the usual brochures, leaflets and annual reports, but there should be an emphasis on meeting face to face to inspire (not simply inform) and encourage advocacy for the library. Do not assume an introduction to the library when a stakeholder is elected onto the council or joins the library as a member of staff will be enough for effective marketing. There is a need to have each of these stakeholders very clearly noted in the annual tactical action plan, with specific marketing and promotional activities directed towards each group during the year.

Even after all that thought, before moving to creating the perfect 'copy' for an advertising or promotional campaign it is important to reflect upon just why the communication is important. Remember each segment may need a different message, perhaps even a different tone of voice in the material, so there cannot be one perfect promotional campaign. It is also important to be clear on whether the communications are to people who already know us or whether they are with people who know very little about us. If the intended recipients of the marketing communications know the library well already, the message may be one of reminding them of what is on offer. This will require a very different message tone from that required if the recipients have no positive experience of the library and need to be informed of what the library is offering and, if there is an expectation that they will come into the library or use services remotely, not just inform them but positively persuade them to try the library. The marketing communication for persuasion is very different from that for reminding existing users of the services on offer.

Communications to support retention and acquisition strategies

Whatever combination of informing, reminding and persuading (Figure 7.1, overleaf) you decide to employ in your marketing communications, it is important to have an appropriate output. Taking a few examples from both user retention (user) and user acquisition (non-user) strategies noted earlier, it is time to consider what the relevant approach to marketing communication should be.

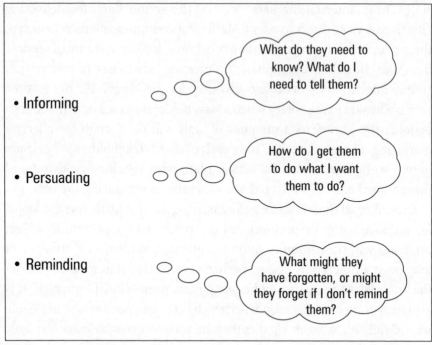

- Informing

What do they need to
know? What do I
need to tell them?

- Persuading

How do I get them
to do what I want
them to do?

- Reminding

What might they
have forgotten, or might
they forget if I don't remind
them?

Figure 7.1   Marketing communications

One user retention strategy may be to ensure that existing local studies users do not forget that the library has a very wide range of general history books in another department which may well add to their understanding and enjoyment of their favourite subjects. Family historians may, after the initial trawl for names, wish to add texture to their understanding by reading about the social background to their ancestors' lives. Marketing communications with this group will be mainly about informing them of the other books on their topic. There may be an element of reminding and persuading, but the general thrust will be to inform. Note that the most important question to ask with an informing marketing communication is not 'What do I want and need to tell them?' but rather 'What do *they* want and need to know?'

Take another group – general fiction readers. If transactional data suggests that most readers take out less than 50% of their entitlement at a time you may sense a quick issues win by simply reminding users that they can take out more books at a time. Clearly this may be a complex issue in reality (will more at a time mean less frequent visits, for instance?), but if it is thought appropriate to communicate this to readers, then the thrust will be mainly reminding, provided that they have been informed of their entitlement when they joined. Note that reminding is a more personal communication than informing, and the copy for any campaign should reflect this. Also note that to identify a fruitful area for reminding users you will benefit from asking yourself: 'What might they have forgotten?' or even 'What might they be in danger of forgetting?' Reminding is an important marketing communication if handled sensitively and not overdone. No one wants to be constantly reminded of anything so use this in areas where quick wins can be expected.

A third group will show the importance of using stronger communication techniques – non-users. Simply informing non-users of the library facilities, collections and services on offer will hopefully attract some new patrons, particularly in areas where they can make a clear and immediate connection between your offer and how it helps them to achieve things of value to them. For instance, alerting non-users to free internet access at the public library was very successful in the early days of England's People's Network. The offer was clear and the benefits easily communicated and understood. This helped libraries to achieve a good level of visitors. Communication aimed at attracting new book readers, though, may need to be more persuasive than simply informative. Not all people will understand just what the library's offer is here, perhaps simply because they do not recognize it as free, or maybe because they really are not aware of the range of materials covered by the modern public library service. However, others will not borrow books because they simply do not see how books can help them achieve things of importance to them. In such instances the marketing communications message will need to have a fair degree of persuasion as well as information. At the very least it will need to explain the benefits the library service brings and most importantly frame these benefits in terms that the user would recognize, not as professionals would describe them.

Developing a contact management strategy

Having decided on our stance towards each key segment, we now develop a contact management strategy to reflect this. Modern marketing recognizes that the world is awash with marketing messages and many of these will simply not have any impact among the sea of other messages. More worryingly, many consumers have a very negative attitude towards mass-marketing efforts. Advertising and promotional activity can damage reputation as well as build a brand.

So how will the library communicate with these segments? There are two strategic options if communication is to stimulate usage. These are termed push and pull strategies.

- A *push strategy* is directed toward the intermediaries that can give the library access to chosen segments or who can influence their feelings about, and attitudes to, the library. If this is agreed to be the best strategy (e.g. for teenagers), then marketing communications and promotions must give an incentive to these 'intermediaries' to encourage and influence use of the public library.
- A *pull strategy*, on the other hand, is directed toward the ultimate user. The focus is on creating demand from the actual user rather than through the influence of intermediaries. This is likely to take a personal tone.

The challenge for the public librarian is to get the message across in a way that has impact but is not intrusive, and this will require an appropriate mix of push and pull strategies. A responsible marketer will have reflected upon the following questions.

1 *How often should the user be contacted?* There is no mathematical formula for this and indeed the right answer is not to be found in a committee sitting around in a smoke-filled room working out the most appropriate figure. The answer is 'As often as the user wants to be contacted!' Users should define their own contact strategies by being given the opportunity to tell the library how often, and when, they

would like to be contacted. In modern marketing language this is an example of customer-managed relationships. The ideal time to gain this information is as part of the joining procedure where there is the opportunity to explore the sort of relationship the user wants with the library. Those who want regular contact should be made contact with regularly; those who want no marketing messages should not be troubled by these. There is no halfway house here which is likely to be both effective and ethical. Seth Godin in his *Permission Marketing* (Simon and Schuster, 1999) notices the difference between this mass marketing approach, or interruption marketing, and a more relationship-based approach, or permission marketing.

2 *Should library marketing communications be general or 'event driven'?* General communications are those sent as a generalized message to all users and potential users. The advantage of these is that a very large number of people can be reached. The disadvantage is that general communications may not reach the user or non-user at a time when they are susceptible to the library message. Think of your own personal experience. Have you occasionally bought something because the message came just at the right time? And how many general messages have you stored in your mind, other than as a vague impression, which you will act upon in the near future? Event-driven communications are communications sent at a particular time to reach the user or non-user at a time when they are likely to be interested in the message, or simply when it is really appropriate for them at that time if only they knew about it. At a very general level these are simply communications about time-specific library events such as story times, author visits and so on, but on reflection you will see that this can be much more sophisticated as an approach to marketing communications. Take children becoming teenagers. There comes a point when they are eligible to move from the children's library to the teenage collection or the adult library. This may not be the most important rite of passage in their life but it is certainly a time when the library should use its marketing skills to inform, remind and even persuade the reader that not only is there a collection of materials outside their usual space in the library (informing) but also that it will

help them achieve things of value to them (persuading) at no extra cost (reminding). Or should we just assume that readers will stumble onto the next stage of their relationship with the library? Most good librarians will naturally sense this is the time to inform readers of new things, but without a specific policy to do this there is the potential for losing readers at this point in their life cycle with us as a customer.

The marketing dialogue

Another useful way to think about your communication strategy is the phrase 'speak, listen and build'. Remember, marketing is a dialogue, not simply the library broadcasting a message. For each segment remember that you have to get the conversation started and then keep it going. Anecdotal evidence suggests that public libraries often start conversations then fail to maintain the conversation over time.

When getting the conversation started it is important to have something that interests your user. Don't just talk about yourself in your marketing communications! You may be really excited that you have books and computers, but remember that people like to be asked about themselves. If your market research is totally divorced from your marketing communications then there is a very real danger that you will be tempted to talk about yourself and your services, rather than bring the user or non-user into the conversation by reflecting back your understanding of where they are trying to go in their lives. Your conversation should involve listening for information and teaching the library benefits and facilities in such a way that it becomes obvious not just that they exist but that they genuinely do help the reader get to where he or she wants to go.

Once the conversation is started do not fool yourself that one marketing leaflet or radio interview or newspaper advertisement is enough to win the hearts and minds of your users and non-users. The conversation has to be kept alive. Where public libraries have managed to do this it is possible to point at successful services. One instance of successful relationship building is in local history, where the library often has a close relationship with the user group who help with viral marketing when new things appear.

This conversation needs to be sustained. How often do you immediately act upon marketing activity that comes your way? Occasionally, but often you need to see an advertisement or message a number of times before you feel confident that you are dealing with an organization that is truly offering something needed and of value. If this is the case why should it be different for people seeing the library message? One-off marketing messages are unlikely to have a significant effect on issues. Anyone undertaking a marketing planning process should have an annual marketing communications plan which will ensure that both the reach of the advertising and the frequency it will be seen by segments of interest will be understood and measured. A wise library marketer recognizes that although some users and non-users will react immediately to the library offer, others will need to be informed and persuaded over time.

Public relations, personal selling and sales promotions

So how should we communicate with users and non-users? We have a set of options which can be configured in a communication mix for each segment (Figure 7.2).

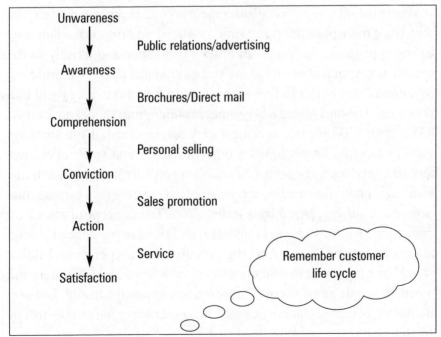

Figure 7.2   Communication mix

The broadest form of marketing communication is public relations. Although this can deliver visits, issues and enquiries from day one, it is best thought of as a long-term process which underpins other communications which seek to directly influence immediate action through either a compelling offer or some sort of incentive to try the service. Often, it is possible to get the local authority's public relations department to undertake this general public relations activity, but you will need to ensure its commitment to this long term. A public library service is rarely, if ever, considered the most important service within local government, and it can be difficult to maintain support for long-term activity in the face of changing departmental priorities.

Public relations can be excellent in building awareness and brand, but will need to be supplemented when those being targeted need to understand just what the library is about and, most importantly, how it helps them to achieve things of value to them. At this point, general public relations may need to be supported by advertising to specific segments, with clear segment-specific messages perhaps rolled out through printed materials or personal visits.

Where the offer to a particular segment is complex then it may require something more powerful than printed material, and personal selling may be the appropriate method – in other words, speaking directly to the specific user group at events where you can not just pass on information or remind them of things they knew already, but also inspire them into library use. Personal selling is very time-consuming and should not be used just to inform people that specific library services exist. If you are using visits and events simply to tell groups of users about your collections, facilities, services and opening hours, then consider just how much this is costing you for the number of people you will reach with a message that perhaps could be carried by a leaflet drop. The concept of return on marketing investment is very important and the cost per contact should always be in your mind. Also the potential impact per pound/dollar should be a key driver in your decision about when to use a brochure and when to speak at an event. Opportunism is always useful, but real marketing planning will not just look for opportunity but temper this by considering potential impact and cost.

There are occasions when the segments you wish to market to already know about your services and need little reminding about the way in which they can access them. They may even be aware of the benefits of using library services. Yet still they do not use them to the extent you would like. In such circumstances they may need a little persuasion to use or increase their usage. For example, a segment of modern fiction readers may have been identified who you believe can be encouraged to take out more books. Perhaps they need a small incentive – a sales promotion would be appropriate. The message communicated to them about their borrowings of modern fiction may include an offer of a free reservation for every three bought (assuming your library charges for reservations). Notice that with sales promotions you can use them in two ways – as a 'bribe' to non-users to try you, or as a 'reward' to existing users to stimulate extra use. Which is the most effective? Anecdotal evidence from librarians who have given away free items, such as a video loan, as a bribe is that this does not work particularly well. As most public libraries seem to be on a user acquisition trail rather than a user retention trail, it is not surprising that most uses of sales promotional methods are as bribes rather than as rewards. The change to recognition of the importance of user retention will encourage more use of sales promotion methods as a reward.

Once users become regular visitors then, as noted earlier in this chapter, we have to enter into a dialogue with them if we wish to maintain some sort of relationship and a claim to be user-centric or user driven. An important part of this communication is to monitor satisfaction levels and, crucially, respond to dissatisfaction with service improvement.

Communications strategy

Once this top-level thinking is in place, a practical communication strategy can be developed. By now you will be aware of the need to have both a general communication strategy for the library and its brand, and a segment communication strategy to ensure that you communicate directly to groups of people with similar needs and wants. The general strategy will create awareness and some degree of familiarity and comfortableness with the concept of a public library and its services. The segment-specific activity will allow you to sell the benefits of public libraries, which will show

how a particular type of user has benefited in the past and how the targeted segment can achieve these benefits. Consider your mix of general and segment-specific messages and note them in the template (Figure 7.3).

General messages to users and non-users	Segment-specific messages to users and non-users
1 2 3	Segment A 1 2 3 Segment B 1 2 3 Segment C 1 2 3

Figure 7.3   Create a set of marketing messages

It is very unlikely that you will be able to undertake the full set of marketing communications you have identified. All public libraries have limited, often very limited, resources for their communication strategy and there is a tendency to look for activities which do many things at once. While one should always be alert to this possibility, there is a real danger of trying to communicate too many messages to too many people through one campaign. If you find yourself deciding marketing activity by committee, beware of the tendency for group think. This will almost certainly compromise the power of your potential messages. Remember that users are looking for things that help them achieve things of value to them, not necessarily what the funding bodies might think that they are funding public libraries for.

Let us move on then to what process we need to keep in mind when creating the message and communicating. Once the set of communications both in general and by segment has been chosen, then a number of key questions arise:

- What shall we say?
- How shall we say it?
- What should the users think?
- What should they do?

Underpinning this thinking is the concept of AIDA – a flow of outcomes from our communications: grabbing users' Attention, developing their Interest, awakening their Desire to use the library and, finally, stimulating their Action, use of the library.

For each communication be aware which part of AIDA is being addressed. Each will require different content (What shall we say?) and tone (How shall we say it?). Over a year we might have sent our target segment a series of messages which takes them along this path. While it is not impossible to take a person from unawareness to action with one campaign, this is not easy and requires an overwhelmingly compelling offer, highly tailored to their needs, so that they instinctively see the benefits of the offer to them and are willing and able to make the immediate effort to do something about it. When thought of in such terms it becomes clear that in most cases users will need to be exposed to a series of messages before any action on their part can be expected. Sending out a leaflet on the Wednesday and then putting extra staff on to cope with the influx on Saturday is not really a marketing communications strategy which you can expect to be successful.

When creating marketing communications there are many factors which need to be taken into account. For each intended communication some thought needs to be given to:

- *Why?* What are we trying to do with this communication? Is it realistic and achievable? Have we been overconfident in our assessment of probable impact? Have we any evidence from other campaigns in public libraries (either ours or in other authorities) that this works?
- *Who?* Have we clearly targeted who is to receive this message?
- *What?* Is the message we intend to communicate clear in our minds?
- *Where?* Do we know which media we are going to use? Direct mail? Radio? In-library display?
- *How?* Will our message be communicated by text or pictures? Will the tone be serious or humorous? Will it be general or be based upon testimonials from other readers who have received the benefits our message will communicate?
- *When?* When is the appropriate time of year to run each message? How many times should we get the message out per year?
- *How much?* Are we clear on the costs of the communications?
- *Schedule.* Have we planned the activity over a one-year integrated planning framework to ensure that we create the weight of advertising required to have significant impact?
- *Response.* Have we considered the potential responses and how to deal with them? For instance, if new users are to be encouraged, do we have the necessary welcome packs and supporting relationship marketing materials?
- *Evaluation.* All of this activity will have expended significant staff effort and have incurred direct costs too. Are we monitoring the costs in time and money to undertake these activities, and tracking the responses to enable the calculation of some degree of return on marketing investment? Marketing communications should not simply be an act of faith.

Making an impact

Given that funds for marketing are inevitably limited in most public library authorities, it is important to identify marketing communications activities which can have a long-lasting impact or ability to create some degree of awareness over time. How can we maximize the marketing potential of those who attend? As an example, a library event may be an excellent way to show the community just how important the library is in the cultural life of the area. An excellent event attended by 50 people will create much goodwill and the right set of thoughts in those who attended. However, in our example, only 50 people attend, despite wide publicity. How can we leverage this? Well, hopefully these 50 people will tell their friends how good an event this was. Such viral marketing is proving very effective in these times of an overproduction of marketing messages. We might even think of ways to encourage readers to talk among themselves about the library. Some of the greatest marketing successes of our times have been built on a first-class product surrounded by viral marketing buzz. To prove the point, just consider your response to 'What is the best search engine?' Given that some will say it depends upon what you want to do, the most popular response will almost certainly be Google. And how much advertising have you seen from Google? Very little. Nevertheless the buzz around Google has been excellent viral marketing. Recently, Google has introduced a newsletter specifically for librarians – an excellent way to understand one important user group and communicate specific messages to a group which can further its claim to be significant in the organization of the world's knowledge.

A long list of marketing communications options is shown below:

- Annual reports
- Articles in the press and local magazines
- Banners on websites and buildings to publicize library events
- Billboards and outside poster advertising
- Bookmarks as a simple reminder
- Brochures to convey the atmosphere in a library
- Bus advertising to get good geographical coverage
- Car-park tickets with printed advertisements or promotions
- Celebrity endorsements of the value of the library
- Classified advertisements in telephone and other directories as a source of reference to users
- Competitions to introduce the fun elements into our communications
- Direct mail to target our message

- Displays to show our wares
- Editorials to position the library as important
- E-mail to develop relationships with users
- Events to put energy and movement into the library offer
- Exhibitions
- Inserts with local authority staff payslips as an example of targeted communications
- Leaflets about service
- Letters to the editor to show library viewpoints
- Networking to keep alert to changing user-needs and opportunities to serve
- Newsletters to provide an ongoing dialogue with users
- Newspaper advertisements to publicize events
- 'Outreach' visits by staff
- Postcards as a way to reinforce a more general message
- Posters displayed in library
- Posters displayed in non-library premises (e.g. leisure facilities, adult education centres, shopping centres, health centres, buses, railway stations)
- Press releases to manage a relationship with the press
- Public service announcements on radio as a general communication
- Public speaking to inspire library use
- Publishing to show expertise
- Radio advertisements as a general communication and brand building
- Signs to direct and emphasize
- SMS (short message service) for permission marketing (see below)
- Stands at shows and fairs to have library presence at key community events
- Telemarketing to help widen library reach or develop relationships with existing users
- Television advertisements – expensive and unlikely, but where negotiated can offer an opportunity to show the creativity of the library
- User testimonials to show evidence of value
- Videos of past library events to show energy

- Visits to schools, playgroups, colleges, local organizations, community groups, business organizations
- Website to inform, remind and inspire
- Welcome pack to create a good first impression
- Word of mouth to generate viral buzz.

It is appropriate to use a combination of many of these, and other, options under a single integrating banner or campaign. In 'The Smartest Card' campaign by the Public Library Association in the US many of these are integrated, including posters, toolkits, celebrity endorsement and news releases. Local libraries produce specific brochures and attend local events to ensure the message is communicated. A combination of approaches is appropriate to convey the message that of all the cards in your wallet, the library card is the most valuable to you.

Innovation has brought with it a number of new technologies to help in marketing activity. Currently mobile marketing appears to have much to offer. SMS, or 'texting', can alert people to when new books come into stock, inform them of events and special offers and even be a quick check of opinion in a market research context. However, such marketing needs to be undertaken with care, as receiving a text message is not always appreciated. As with most other kinds of effective marketing, mobile marketing should be based upon permission marketing principles – users should sign up to receive messages or not be sent them, regardless of their current relationship with the library. An addition to the library joining card is a good example of an appropriate form to use in order to implement this. With non-users, permission should be collected directly from them in such a way that they are clear that they are on a mobile marketing list. Despite the caution that should be exercised here it is clear that, undertaken sensitively, mobile marketing is a highly appropriate tactic in your strategic marketing plan to attract priority segments such as teenagers.

Return on marketing communications investment

There are clearly many potential marketing options for public libraries.

Whatever combination of approaches is finally considered best to meet the marketing objectives, be sure to make this decision based upon the return you will get for your marketing spend. Although some marketing is undertaken for general brand building, it is not wise to think of marketing as simply a good thing in itself that does not require detailed and specific measurement. Like all library activities there are costs associated with marketing, and where money or effort is spent you should be looking to show a good return for that.

There are three important concepts to help you judge the most economical way to achieve your marketing objectives:

- *reach*: calculate the number of different target users/potential users who are exposed to a message at least once during a specific period of time
- *frequency*: calculate the number of times an individual is exposed to a given message during a specific period of time
- *cost per contact*: from reach, frequency and the cost of the communication it is possible to calculate the cost of reaching one member of the target market. This is a useful benchmark figure to use for subsequent planning rounds.

If these key marketing measurement concepts are kept firmly in mind there is every chance that you will be able to make good decisions on the type of approaches to take in your marketing efforts. These cost-per-contact figures can be useful in inter-authority comparisons.

Of course, you need to be effective as well as economical and efficient. Indeed, being efficient and economical but totally ineffective is not a good use of time or money even if the reach, frequency and cost per contact figures are impressive. The expected outcome of any marketing activity is that users and non-users will do more of what you wanted them to do when you started to think about your marketing. If they do not, then no inter-authority comparisons on marketing costs can have any impact except in the political arena. The political arena is very important to the future funding of public library services, but it should be remembered that the interests of users and the interests of politicians are not always the same.

Will users and non-users respond to library communications?

You can lead a horse to water but you can't make it drink. Remember this. Your marketing activity can inform, remind and even persuade, but you still have to meet user or non-user objections to your offer, and you may not be close enough to your readers to be aware of what these are. Often the main barrier to surmount will be apathy. If you have undertaken the value analysis suggested earlier in this book then it is to be hoped that apathy will not be a significant hurdle – you will be providing something of value to users now, not just something that is vaguely interesting to them at some point in the future.

Assuming that you have created a good marketing strategy based on achieving specific marketing objectives, turned that strategy into a series of well-chosen activities over a year and assessed the likely reach, frequency and cost per contact, then your temptation to sit back and breathe a sigh of relief as it rolls out should be tempered with a nagging worry – it is fine in theory, but what will happen in practice?

Even if the strategy is executed well and all the activities happen on time, in full, there will still be a number of barriers that your message may meet. These are some of the negative comments which may arise:

- *I don't believe you.* Before you run your campaign be honest with yourself. Is the communication about something which you can realistically deliver? Will the users or non-users have different experiences of the library from what is offered in our publicity and promotions? Put bluntly, will they believe that the library can deliver its promise?
- *I don't need it.* Is the library truly offering things which users and non-users perceive to be of value? Do they really need it? Are we acting as social engineers telling them that they need it?
- *I don't have enough time.* When they read or see library publicity, are users and non-users likely to reject the offer because it is just not convenient? Have we communicated not just that it is valuable in helping them get to where they want to go, but also that it is easily accessed in ways that are convenient to them?

- *I don't have enough money.* Has the message of the true cost of the library service been communicated? Public librarians are still often amazed at the number of new users or potential users who expect the library to charge for the service. Do marketing messages reflect how much the user is expected to pay for service? Remember that 'I don't have enough money' might include the travel costs to the library. Has this potentially hidden cost been taken into account when creating marketing communications?

- *It won't work for me.* Is there any evidence in the publicity that it will work for the user in particular? Nothing communicates faster than the experience of someone the user can relate to. From our earlier discussion of the importance of segmentation (Chapter 4) it is clear that if only general library benefits are communicated in publicity material then there is the distinct possibility that the message will not gain the attention it seeks.

If your current messages and promotions cannot meet these five basic objections above, then do not expect users to rush through the door or whatever else you wanted them to do. Remember that although there may be good answers to these objections, if they are not dealt with as part of the marketing campaign potential users may never come close enough to the library for library staff to have an opportunity to meet their objections. It is very dangerous to assume that the library simply needs to inform users and non-users of library services and as a consequence they will immediately understand the benefits to them personally.

Marketing communications at different stages of the user life cycle

A further complication to effective marketing communication arises from the user life cycle introduced in Chapter 6 (Figure 6.7, page 127). Some specific marketing and communications activities at each stage of the user life-cycle are as follows:

1 *Wish for.* At this early stage the important marketing activities are targeting, segmentation (based on an understanding of users' or non-

users' needs, wants and, most importantly, the value that a public library can bring to them on their terms on their journey through life) and lifetime value calculations. Targeting users will always be driven partly by political imperatives and partly by more general performance indicators. For the latter it will be very important to understand the lifetime values (i.e. the number of issues, visits, etc. they might be able to offer over the lifetime of their existence as library users) of particular segments to help choice of effort to be made. Marketing messages should look to reflect the diversity rather than to provide a single message.

2   *First response*. When non-users respond to first marketing messages it is important that an effective enquiry management process or system is in place with supporting standards of response. Sometimes a local authority will have a call centre.

3   *Becoming a user*. Once non-users make their first tentative step to visit the library, there is an opportunity to get the relationship off to a good start by having appropriate welcoming procedures, perhaps including a welcome pack. For those libraries who have grasped this opportunity to get to understand a little about what users are likely to use the library for, there is a chance to offer a highly individual welcome pack based upon the specific interests of the user or the segments he or she is a member of.

4   *Exchanging information*. As users visit the library they leave a trail of transactions which can be used in a marketing context to help the library understand either the way the service operates in general or, more specifically, how individual users use the library, with the consequent opportunity to tailor services. This is known as database marketing (DBM). DBM should underpin all specific marketing communications.

5   *Exchanging goals*. As the relationship between library and user develops, one of the most important things to emerge is trust. Users who have had a good experience of library responsiveness, and responsible use of personal data you hold, may well trust you more and more with information about themselves. Some will allow you to use this to tailor the service to them because they believe their data is safe with you and

you will use it responsibly to their benefit. To do this with new users is less realistic, as a climate of trust has not been developed at that early stage of the relationship.

6   *Dealing with problems.* At any one time, even in the most efficient of libraries, there will be users who feel that the service given is not what they would expect and there is potential to lose such people with all the visits, issues and enquiries they contribute towards your performance measures. Effective marketing will be aware of users at risk and manage accordingly. Complaint-handling procedures will be in place.

7   *Loss/recovery.* Good marketers will not simply shrug their shoulders as users desert their libraries. Procedures will be in place for understanding reasons for lost or lapsed readers and welcoming back lost customers as a result of marketing communications and campaigns.

Consider appropriate communications by populating the grid in Figure 7.4 with specific communications you could devise at specific stages of the user life cycle. Note that not all communications options will be appropriate at each stage of the life cycle. For example, dealing with loss or recovery is more likely to benefit from a personal or telephone approach than one of the other approaches.

	Personal contact	Direct mail	Advertising	Telephone	Web/ e-mail
Wish for					
First contact					
Becoming a user					
Exchange information					
Deal with problems					

Figure 7.4   Communications during the user life cycle

Producing marketing communications materials

Marketing communications (marcoms) can take a number of forms according to whether the communications will be event-specific or general, to be used as and when appropriate, or to be communications to all or to a specific segment.

Consider each of the four options shown in Figure 7.5.

	General interest	Segment-specific
Stock marcoms		
Event-specific marcoms		

Figure 7.5   Ensuring an appropriate set of marketing communications

1   *Stock marcoms with general interest.* These will be information leaflets and similar communications approaches. The messages will tend to inform or remind the recipient about the range of services available via the library service. Such marcoms will include fact sheets, press releases, a contact list for the media and case studies of how the library has made a difference to people's lives. Do you have a media kit which can be sent out on demand to the local newspaper or radio station? Perhaps you have even made it available via your website? If not, you should consider this as journalists are occasionally pushed by deadlines and quick access to information can be the difference between being mentioned and not mentioned.

Another type of stock marcom with general interest is the slogan. Slogans grab the attention of the user and have the potential to position the library in the user's or non-user's mind in some way. In the US, for instance, the Public Library Association committed itself to the Campaign for America's Libraries by adopting the slogan 'The Smartest Card. Get it. Use it. @your library', with a three-year programme to make the library card 'the most valuable card in your wallet'. This is an engaging slogan which can be used regularly as an attention grabber if not, of itself, sufficiently targeted to have direct impact on habits. Such slogans can provide an umbrella for more targeted campaigns.

2   *Stock marcoms with segment-specific messages.* Such communications will outline the value of particular products and services to particular segments. For example, a general leaflet for 'silver surfers' may be produced and used for occasional campaigns to this segment. Messages about access to the internet will be similar to those directed at other segments, but will also stress the patient help at hand as well as other factors which are deemed to be particularly important to this segment.

3   *Event-specific marcoms for general use.* These marcoms will be useful for general brand building, but are unlikely to inspire immediate library use. They will give information on key library features such as opening hours and types of material on offer, and may talk about the general benefits of using the library. However they will not be specific enough to appeal to particular library segments. They will differ from stock marcoms in that, although containing similar information, the layout, design and perhaps a small amount of the text has been customized to reflect the event.

4   *Event-specific marcoms for particular segments.* These highly targeted marcoms will reflect both the segment needs and the characteristics of the event. An example would be materials for when children become teenagers – a significant event with implications for library use.

Create a media kit

A thorough approach to marcoms will ensure that you have marketing messages and communications which are ready for a range of applications. When the radio or newspaper wants material, the library should be able to respond to this quickly and efficiently. You should know how you are going to deal with approaches from the media to get the best out of such contacts for the public library. Are there real human stories among library publicity material, for example? A press release or stock story which includes details of how an individual used the library and benefited from it greatly (in their terms!) is a far more attractive item to the media than an informational leaflet finely crafted by committee.

Of course, good marketing is proactive and waiting for the media to decide to contact us is not particularly dynamic. There is a need to identify opportunities and make sure that the library has a dedicated spokesperson to respond. Identify opportunities to contact the media with stories they can run. Libraries should make news. This does not have to be at the level of how libraries have saved the world – as noted earlier, some of the more interesting stories are those that involve human interactions with the library. A good library marketer will not only have identified the contacts in the local media but will have a good idea of the sort of stories each contact has been involved with and their current issues. Given the broad remit of the public library there is a very good chance that the library can support any issue which arises, provided that this support is acceptable to the set of library stakeholders.

Cast your mind back to when you last read your local newspaper. What attracted you most? For many of us it will be the either joyous or sad stories of people's lives rather than the business stories of the new machinery installed at the local postal sorting office. There are many joyous stories around public libraries which are not currently promoted. Such stories are part of our stock of evidence supporting our worth to the community. By using the library Mr Jones found his long-lost brother. Mrs Smith consulted an antiques guide in the library to find she had a very exciting and valuable item; having sold it she was then able to go on a once in a lifetime voyage around the world. A teenager became a sound engineer after being inspired by the rock band who played at a library event and reading the relevant books in the library and more provided by interlibrary loans. This is the character of good marketing: not a simple leaflet outlining the number of books and PCs on offer, or the opening hours. Communicate inspiration rather than simply information.

There is no one perfect set of promotional materials. Consider all the opportunities you might have for getting the message out there. Has the library created a set of marketing communications materials which will cover all these opportunities? Chapter 4 should have convinced you that one size will not fit all and that you should be as careful in segmenting the intermediaries and media as you are in segmenting your user and non-user base.

Create a media kit if you do not have one already. Not only will this be a useful resource but the exercise of creating it will force you to think about what you are trying to say to the world. To simply react when approached will encourage bland responses which in turn may not be sufficiently interesting to use. If, for instance, you have not collected real library success stories it is unlikely you will immediately offer such items when approached one hour before the journalist's deadline.

The media kit should include brochures, fact sheets, photographs, a listing of key contacts in the library who can act as spokespersons on specific topics, and copies of any logos or other graphic material that can be used in the newspaper to help with library branding. Include case studies and some general quotes attributable to individuals in the library. Most importantly this media kit should be reviewed annually as part of the marketing planning process: out-of-date contacts and quotes will do more harm than good.

Writing copy for your marketing communications

Librarians would not claim great copywriting skills as part of their professional education. At the same time marketing effort is rarely supported by sufficient funds to employ professional copywriting consultants, although the local authority public relations and media relations department may have some skill in-house. Even here demands on their time may mean that such access to expertise is denied in favour of other, larger, local authority departments.

In such circumstances public library staff should be aware of some basic practical principles on writing effective copy. Effective copy will be relevant (the ideas must have resonance with those who are to receive the messages), original and impactful. Some of the key things to remember when writing copy are:

1 *Make sure you are succinct and keep focus.* Every word matters. There is such a thing as too much information. Be aware of what you are trying to do, and do not try to do too many things at once with your marketing communication.

2 *Try to be very specific.* Address your segment of interest and not some idea of a general reader out there. There is, of course, no such general reader.

3 *Get personal.* Do not forget that if your copy has 'human interest' it is more likely to gain attention. A good way to include a personal dimension is to try to include real testimonials from such people. Your copy should not just claim benefits for your service but should show how real people have received those benefits from the library and would recognize them as benefits.

4 *Try to look for some original angle.* For example, look for an unexpected twist or association, or a play on words or catchy phrase. Analogies and metaphors can also add interest to a message. Beware, though, of over-clever slogans which have little or any content when challenged but sound good around the senior management table. The original angle needs to be in the users' or non-users' experience, and they are very familiar with slogans.

5 *Use the language of conversation.* You want a response so that there is a dialogue. Keep the language such that it feels like a response is needed. Remember the end of many marketing communications is action by the user or non-user. If your part of the conversation does not need a response, then why will they bother to give one?

It is important to be clear on what message format you are going to use the text in. A *straightforward* format will simply be based on an informational message. If you are using a *demonstration* format, the message will be about how to use the service. A *comparison* format will show how the library is the best place to undertake a particular research or other activity. Sometimes the message will be about *how to solve a problem* – the library might be seen as the solution to a search for suppliers of a particular product, for instance. *Endorsement* can be a useful format if you have celebrities to help build credibility.

Using a call centre

Some library authorities will use a call centre, contact centre or customer interaction centre as part of the management of marketing communications. Often this will not be a library-specific centre but part use of an authority-wide facility. Such an approach has the opportunity to provide a smooth transaction for the user or the ability to damage relationships with users who are disappointed by the experience.

There are two options for managing library marketing communications through a call centre. Inbound calls can be received and filtered to the appropriate department. Outbound calls can be made via call-centre staff for general telemarketing or specific projects, such as contacting lapsed users.

Your website as a marketing communication

What does your website communicate (not 'what do you intend your website to communicate')? To ensure clarity of communication and usability it is important to test website changes before going live.

Marketing is, as we noted in Chapter 1, a dialogue over time. As such we should take the opportunity to enrich this dialogue through the library website. In addition to pages of information about the library and its services, library users and non-users should be offered feedback and comment forms. Remember that users need a reason to revisit the website, and you can increase these reasons by introducing features based on new technologies as they arise. Remain alert to these and apply technology to help reinforce the library brand as energetic and modern.

Current technologies which may prove useful to readers include RSS. RSS ('rich site summary' or 'really simple syndication') and weblogs will allow the library to offer a news update service to those wishing to be kept informed of library events and developments. This is particularly useful as it allows people to have library news collated with all the other things their RSS reader integrates. The library becomes part of their life, which is one of the key objectives of marketing activity.

Weblogs offer an opportunity for the library service to keep the website vibrant and worth revisiting regularly. Such weblogs can either be general about the library services and developments, or can be segment- or service-specific, such as a weblog for teenagers or users of the local history collection. Whatever its basis, the weblog can provide an important and vibrant communication channel with users or interested non-users.

Personalization of the user's experience of the website so that each person can access a different home page customized to their needs is now a realistic option. However, personalization is not always a positive experience for website users and may not be worth the effort needed to establish the infrastructure.

Finally, recognize that the website is a way to extend the communication you make with users or non-users. Consider videoing events run in the library. Permissions will need to be obtained, but it is well worth while making the effort. A video of the event can be made accessible as a simple click on the library website and is a constant reminder of the energy in the library service. It is also extra content for the website which with significant offline marketing of the event can draw visitors.

Promotional activity

When confident that you have a sound set of marketing communications and advocacy materials to help inform, remind or persuade your users and non-users, there may still be little doubt in the back of your mind that these will be sufficient to inspire the library usage you seek as part of your marketing plan. It may be that you need to be a little more persuasive just to kick-start library use.

Public libraries are able to utilize a range of promotional activities that for-profit organizations offer. As noted earlier, promotions can be used as either 'bribes' (e.g. to non-users to try the library) or as 'rewards' (e.g. to thank users for their patronage and to encourage even more usage).

Here are two examples of a promotion as a 'bribe':

- The New York Public Library (NYPL) has a library shop (www. thelibraryshop.org) which includes a whole range of appropriate materials for sale. This is very much tied in with the general public library activities: a NYPL bookmark notes 'Become a member of the New York Public Library today and receive a 10% discount on all of your purchases at The Library Shop'.
- Registering for the Children's Summer Reading Programme in Dunedin Library (New Zealand) entitles the person who registers to a free video/DVD voucher.

Here are two examples of a promotion as a 'reward':

- Tameside (UK) has a reward card. The reward is the chance to exchange points for a normally charged library service. Each time a user uses the library to borrow books, videos, CDs or talking books, a member of staff stamps the card. Only one stamp per day is allowed, and each stamp = 1 point. Points can be exchanged for: free reservations of items in stock (4 points per item); free 30 minute sessions on the internet (4 points per session); loans of CDs or talking books (8 points each); loans of videos and DVDs (non-reservable videos and DVDs can only be borrowed from the library where they are stocked) and language tapes (12 points each). Full reward cards go into a draw for a book token.
- Members of Friends of the Library in Kansas City, USA, receive up to two free videos every visit and one admittance to opening night of the Annual Book Lover's Book Sale.

Less exciting promotional approaches, yet still worth using as supporting materials, are printed table tents (printed cards folded into the shape of a tent, to be left on surfaces and ledges in the library), badges, notepads, pens, promotional gifts, balloons, frisbees and a host of other items suitably embellished with appropriate logos and graphics. More useful perhaps is free car parking time for library users when using the library. Library suppliers and national organizations (e.g. in the UK www.literacytrust.org.uk) often have downloadable printed promotional materials. In addition to national organizations some regional public libraries (e.g. see Alberta Libraries, www.visityourlibrary.net) also have free materials to browse online and download. Although these will often be specific to individual library authorities they are a good source of ideas for your own promotional activity.

It is often possible to 'piggyback' on national initiatives such as a national reading day and gain the benefits of centrally produced marketing communications and promotional activity. However, it is possible to overemphasize support for national initiatives at the expense of undertaking deep, highly specific marketing communications and promotions with your local users and non-users.

After all this effort it would be nice to relax but the marketing communications must be completed with a set of internal communications to ensure all staff understand the messages sent out and the expected range of responses they will need to deal with. Internal communication methods will include face-to-face communications, newsletters, letters, notes, memos, notice boards and e-mail. Do not forget to tailor messages to each stakeholder group. Remember that you have to inspire them to support the ideas behind the marketing communications to users and non-users. Simply informing stakeholders of the communications sent out is not enough.

Now that you have a strategy (Chapters 5 and 6) and a marketing communications programme (this chapter), attention now turns to implementation of the plan in the next chapter.

Reflecting upon your marketing communications:

- Have you a clear idea of which user segments should receive which messages when?
- Do you have a well-thought-out integrated communications strategy and mix of alternative approaches?
- Are your communications appropriate for the objectives they are expected to achieve?
- Are you measuring the impact of your communications to identify what works and what doesn't?
- Are you ready for the media when they contact you?
- Is your promotional activity a good mix of bribes and rewards?

Chapter 8

Implementation and quick progress

By the end of this chapter you will be aware of how to make quick progress despite the constraints on effective marketing planning. You will recognize the importance of 'quick wins' in keeping energy within the process. Advice is also offered on action and resource plans, monitoring the plan and staffing for marketing planning.

Having undertaken the analytical part of marketing planning and chosen a set of key strategies and marketing communications, attention can be given to what should be the most satisfying part of the marketing planning process - implementation and the pride in return from marketing effort. Although this is potentially the most satisfying part of the marketing planning process it can be the most frustrating if new priorities appear early in the plan's timescale which deflect attention from long-term strategic planning.

Barriers to implementation

One of the major barriers to effective strategic marketing planning is the difficulty in implementation. Staff may recognize the need for marketing, but it is important that for effective implementation this recognition is supported by an atmosphere in which staff and other stakeholders feel the plan is to their personal advantage. It is important to have top management commitment, but in addition modern leadership recognizes that simply ordering staff to implement is not always the most appropriate way to get things done. Without this feeling of personal advantage for all there is a danger that the best laid plans will, for a variety of often good reasons, not materialize. Some of the common responses by those on front-line teams who have to implement marketing plans in all types of organizations are:

- It means more work
- We tried it before
- It's just a fad
- It might cost money
- We already know our users
- There might not be much in it, so it might not be worth the effort
- Lots of other reasons!

When advocating your plan throughout the organization remember to make sure that you have met these and any other local objections. This will require leadership and change-management skills, because strategic marketing plans almost always involve change. Change is at the very least disorientating and, at worst, positively frightening for employees. Once set on the path of implementing a strategic marketing plan the team needs to show not just commitment but also nerve. They will not do this unless persuaded that the judgement behind the marketing plan is sound. Internal marketing is key. Library staff at all levels of hierarchy should clearly understand how important the proposed marketing activity is if the public is to receive all the benefits of the library service. Furthermore they should be aware of just how important their contribution is to the unfolding plan. Note that to do this requires more than simply telling staff that they are important.

Assuming that the front-line staff are fully ready, willing and able to play their part in the roll-out of the marketing plan, it is still wise to be aware of other things which can derail your plan. The plan should be broken down into manageable components to ensure that the implications for staff on a day-to-day basis are clear. The initial strategic thinking will require a detailed action plan which can be project-managed to ensure good integration of the various actions. Manage the expectations of staff. Be realistic. It is easy to underestimate the amount of time it takes to get certain effects, and overambition can lead to a lack of confidence in marketing when the expected results do not materialize quickly.

Internal marketing is important if the grand ideas in the marketing plan are to roll out. It is possible to think of marketing as the responsibility of everyone within the public library system. If this is your view, then internal marketing of the marketing plan – treating your staff as customers for the plan – is vital to ensure than the user is kept front of mind by all library staff. Beware, however, that to simply offer the glib statement that 'Marketing is the responsibility of everyone' is unlikely to be a rallying cry if it is perceived as simply one more thing to do on top of an already busy week and high workload. Marketing does not 'just happen', and specific resources and time must be allocated to it if it is to achieve its aims. This does not have to be a large proportion of the library budget, but it does need to be regular and consistent.

Managing team and user expectations

In the early stage of marketing planning there is likely to have been excitement and expectation among the team involved. Marketing is fun. It is usually about growth and change, and allows creative thinking. As a process, marketing planning creates options, and challenges existing priorities. Expectations need to be managed within resources and what can be achieved within timescales. Returns from strategic marketing do not happen overnight: it is an iterative learning process. 'Quick wins' will keep energy in the process.

Similarly your planning activities will create expectations in users and non-users. Do not underestimate the critical importance of first impressions when users or non-users respond to your marketing activities. It is an old saying that you never get a second chance to make a first impression.

During implementation of the plan ensure that you manage the expectations it creates for both those it intends to serve and those responsible for delivering it. Challenge your plans and the way you manage their implementation.

1 *Do you provide a realistic picture of what users can expect?* Is the library offer clear to users, non-users and staff? Is it clear what can be claimed and what is a reasonable expectation?

2 *Are staff made aware not to promise what can't be delivered?* If, for instance, staff are to offer to call back with the answer to a reference query, then the call should be made within the agreed time. An offer to call back 'later in the morning' when the library is very busy and running under strength is clearly very unlikely to happen. It is better to under-promise and over-deliver in implementation. Remember that if informed 'later in the morning' then the user may build this into their day. Similarly, if erring on the side of caution a response is promised 'By the time the library closes today', then the user has the opportunity to plan his or her day differently. And when the library does manage to deliver the answer late morning, the impression created is one of delivering above expectations rather than below expectation.

3 *When promoting a service as part of the plan are you always accurate in your description?* If you have set a standard which the library can meet only on a day when everything goes to plan, then it is very likely that expectations will not be met. When creating library publicity materials remember that the description of library services on offer has to be delivered, as far as possible, on time in full. This should be regardless of who is on duty, what time of day the enquiry presents itself and the nature of the enquiry.

4 *Do those who make promises to users and non-users (management) talk to those who deliver (front-line teams in branches)?* Implementation will not be successful if management believe that a certain level of service is possible but are not in a dialogue with branch library staff who know the limitations which might prevent delivery of the offer. Implementation of a marketing plan requires full commitment and belief. There are so many weak points in any plan that management must remain alert to what is happening with the front-line teams.

5 *Do you actively look for where things could go wrong?* The one thing that is known about planning is that things will not go to plan. What are the risks to the implementation of your marketing plan? Resource promises not being fulfilled? Changed priorities three months into the plan? High

staff turnover? If these or other local risks turn into events and issues is the marketing plan compromised? Have you taken into account what you will do if the major risks to the plan become reality? While contingency planning should not take an inordinate amount of time away from the more obviously positive aspects of planning, a wise planner, who recognizes that the benefits of any strategic plan appear gradually, will have some broad thoughts on how to react to unforeseen events. In the absence of this a plan can quickly turn into a crisis or simply fizzle out.

6   *Are staff trained to react to problems or to anticipate problems?* It is unlikely that a plan will be problem-free during implementation, and staff should be briefed to expect issues to arise. The implementation of the plan should be on the agenda at management meetings, and staff should feel able to talk about the risks to the plan without fear that they will be perceived as negative or 'not team players'. To anticipate problems is to provide an opportunity to ensure the plan can be implemented as smoothly as possible.

Managing implementation risks

It is wise to complete any strategy with an implementation risk assessment – 'What will derail implementation of the plan?' There are two useful techniques to help you with this: a risk matrix and a force field analysis.

A risk matrix (Figure 8.1, overleaf) identifies all the risks to the plan and prioritizes those which need immediate attention as opposed to those which should simply be monitored. Risks are negative or positive events which, if they occur, will have an impact on the ability to deliver the plan. If the circumstances which come to mind already exist then they are issues not risks. Issues are managed as part of the general management process; risks are often ignored until it is too late to make easy changes, and a crisis is born.

Risks to the strategic marketing plan might include issues such as staff not being committed to implementation, resources being diverted, or a sudden realignment of priorities. Such items should be plotted on a matrix such as that shown in Figure 8.1, and the advice for each quadrant noted. Issues that plot in the high/high quadrant should be regularly

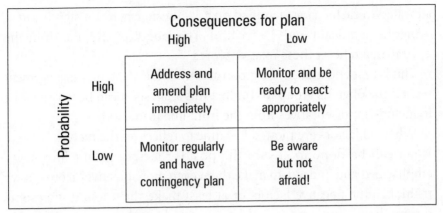

Figure 8.1   A risk matrix

assessed at management team meetings, and these may be worth an agenda item if they are critical to the implementation of the plan. Implementation requires at least as much attention as the earlier stages of devising the strategy and plan.

Another approach, which this time emphasizes the positive influences on the implementation of the marketing plan, is the force field analysis (Figure 8.2). In this analysis the central area is whatever is to be achieved, in this case successful implementation of the library marketing plan. Either side of this area are plotted the positive or negative factors in this endeavour: the negative factors which will potentially stop achievement of a successful implementation and the positive factors which are in support of a successful implementation. Each side has plus or minus scores

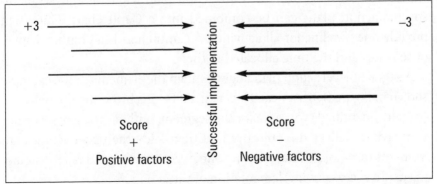

Figure 8.2   Force field analysis: the positive and negative forces on our library marketing plan

allocated to each factor identified on a 1–3 scale where 1 = significant, 2 = highly significant and 3 = critical. The length of the line from the central area reflects these relative scores.

This is best undertaken as a group activity. While the senior management team is the obvious group to conduct this analysis, it can be worth while to include representatives from the front-line teams too.

When all factors are plotted it is time to reflect on the picture created. What can be done to ensure the positive factors in our favour are emphasized and, indeed, to make them even more positive? How can we neutralize the negative factors or at least make them less troublesome during the planning period? When undertaking this exercise note that the most important thing is not how accurate the scoring is but rather how you can influence the forces acting upon your plan implementation.

Action plan

The action plan should comprise the set of activities within the marketing strategies which will, if efficiently and effectively delivered, be sufficient to give the library a reasonable chance of successfully meeting its marketing objectives, whether they be issue, visitor, enquiry or other quantified measure.

There will, of course, be some marketing activities for overall awareness raising and brand building, but, as noted earlier, general messages do not necessarily deliver increases in library use. Segment-specific messages are likely to be far more effective in meeting quantified objectives and it is appropriate to reflect this in your action plan. General and segment-specific action plans can be combined into a Gantt chart which will provide one timeline for all activities. A Gantt chart is a graphic display of activities and the time allocated to them.

A segment-level action plan might contain the elements in the example shown in Figure 8.3, overleaf. Notice that it begins by noting the objective (usually quantified) you have for the segment, outlines the key strategies you have to deliver the objective and then adds the usual action plan elements of actions, timescales, resource requirement and responsibility to ensure successful implementation of the action.

Segment A
Objective: ————
  Strategies:
    1. ————
 	
    2. ————
	Action	Timescale	Resource	Responsibility

	———— ———— ————			
	———— ————			

Figure 8.3   Example action plan

The action plan should be a one-year series of activities which implement the first year of the three-year strategic marketing plan. Using such an approach it is possible to see at a glance whether or not there is a reasonable chance of achieving the objective. Are the actions strong enough to implement fully the strategies which we believe will be strong enough to deliver the amount of activity we desire from the segment? And are those actions over the year well supported by resources with clear responsibilities to ensure completion?

Resource plan

A marketing plan is not simply a repository of good ideas. It is a series of actions which require resources to implement such actions. It is unlikely that any strategic marketing plan can be delivered within existing resources. Marketing is an investment in a desired future outcome and as such will lose a significant amount of impact if the implementation of the plan is not directly resourced with money and staff time specifically allocated to it. Small gains are possible from a 'we'll fit in marketing when we can' approach, but the change of image or impact on whole segments of users or non-users will require a deep commitment. This is a shared responsibility between national and local library authorities.

All marketing activity should be fully costed and resources agreed. As noted earlier, marketing is an investment, not an act of faith. Consequently senior library management has a responsibility to track the return on that investment. In addition to salaries for staff time on marketing, there are many other costs which need to be identified (Figure 8.3). These include training, postage, printing, design and media costs. When these are allocated it is possible, in the context of our marketing objectives (a combination of increases in visits, issues, enquiries, website hits, etc.), to calculate a measure of return on investment. Often these measures will at first be very broad, but as marketing planning develops over a number of planning rounds the relationship between spend and outcome will become clearer and more robust as a planning tool.

Activity	Direct costs	Indirect costs	Total cost of activity

Figure 8.4   Resource requirement

Control and monitoring

It is important to review regularly how the plan is being implemented both in terms of how the return on the investment is going and also how stakeholders feel about the implementation.

Whatever performance measures are chosen to manage marketing activity, remember that they should be relevant to the activity being undertaken and the marketing objectives you have. Good performance measures will monitor progress, encourage appropriate behaviour among library staff, deliver and communicate key information, establish account-abilities and reveal opportunities to improve the service. In addition they will be clear and easily understood by all. Bad performance measures, on the other hand, will be difficult to understand and not deliver enough benefits for the amount of time they take to collect and discuss. They will not encourage appropriate behaviour and will not be directly affected by the work group they are measuring. Bad performance measures will not highlight the things the library needs to know in order to improve.

It is highly likely that the measures and indicators you use to report on your progress towards meeting funding bodies' requirements will need to be supplemented by other measures and indicators to review the success or otherwise of your marketing.

A new library as part of your marketing plan

If you are lucky enough to be able to afford a new library as part of your next marketing plan, remember that it is part of your portfolio and as such needs to be integrated within the marketing plan. It is appropriate to have a detailed action plan of events together with publicity and promotions specifically for the introduction of the new library. However, remember that the strategy for the new library is unlikely to be stand-alone, particularly if it is a new central library. There are implications for the whole network of branches and services.

Here are some important things to consider when introducing a new library as part of a marketing plan.

1 The marketing plan should have action points which pre-date the opening by 12–18 months. There is the opportunity to create 'buzz' by slowly introducing the library over time. Well before opening there can be publicity about the plans, perhaps competitions related to the new library six months before opening and the full range of publicity and promotions as the date nears. Do not forget that it is important to continue marketing after the library has opened. Intensive marketing will be required for at least six weeks after opening and only then can it become part of the general marketing and publicity portfolio. Remember that new buildings can be delayed so there is a need to build some flexibility into your marketing.

2 Ensure the community is involved from the very beginning. Explain the library vision, mission and values to the community. This is all part of the relationship building discussed earlier in this book. If this process is not started early do not expect the community to suddenly become enthusiastic after opening day. Seattle Public Library in the USA began its process by undertaking focus groups with ten 'work

groups', as well as having comments forms available in libraries. These groups were general/recreational library users, researchers, ESL/literacy, homeless, disabled, young adults, children's services, business community, arts community and older adults. Use as many means as possible to allow the community to add their views.

3   Remember that everything is likely to take longer than you think, and will probably cost more than originally budgeted for.

The opening of a new central library should be seen as such an important event for the community that it offers the opportunity for unusual one-off joint promotional activities with other organizations. When Seattle opened its new central library in 2004, free metro rides to the new library were negotiated for opening day. From several weeks before opening residents were able to pick up a free ride ticket, in the form of a bookmark, from any branch library in Seattle or the metro's customer service office. On visiting the library, residents were able to pick up a free return ticket.

Evaluation of marketing effort

After all the effort of developing a marketing strategy and plan, and the stresses and strains of implementing the plan, it is very important to evaluate the impact that the marketing effort has made. This is important for two reasons. First, in most public library contexts there is a need to show that public funds have been spent wisely, and marketing should show a return for the investment in an increase in one or more performance measures. Second, if marketing activities are not evaluated, how will we know what works and what does not? The most effective and efficient marketing will always learn from previous campaigns: evaluation is part of that learning. Evaluation is the starting point in the next round of planning.

After every marketing campaign, ask:

- Did it achieve the goals it set out to meet?
- What worked particularly well?
- What didn't work quite as well as hoped?
- If we were to start this again, what would we have done differently?
- What should be done exactly the same next time?

Wherever possible measure progress by both the way it feels to stakeholders and the quantification of outputs. Make it easy for users and staff to comment on how things are going. Never forget that marketing is to achieve an objective so ensure that you evaluate your marketing effort in such terms whether this is increases in issues, visits or enquiries, or another indicator of performance.

It can sometimes be difficult to evaluate library awareness campaigns as these can be a success even if the issues, visits or enquiries do not immediately increase. Many companies conduct pre- and post-advertising surveys of awareness to identify a baseline and impact measures. However, most public library systems will have done well to generate funding for the campaign, never mind the evaluation stage. It is to be hoped that, as authorities move further towards a marketing orientation, more funds will become available for such evaluation.

Certain library marketing activities will be more easily evaluated than others. Campaigns which focus on drawing visitors to a website will have a natural counting mechanism in the visitor log which is built into most systems. For this reason it might be useful to direct some of the promotional campaigns via the website, particularly those which are aimed at the more computer-literate segments of the library market.

Implementation case study: Norfolk and Norwich Millennium Library

The Norfolk and Norwich Millennium Library in Norfolk, UK, is a flagship development arising from the misfortune of a major central library burning down in 1994. The event, though unwanted, offered the opportunity to create a new central library from scratch. After the initial shock of the loss of a much-loved library, a temporary replacement and a period of reflection over several years enabled new thinking to emerge on what a central library could and should be. The Norfolk and Norwich Millennium Library was to occupy a prominent place alongside local radio and television (not in the original but included later), a learning centre, Tourist Information, restaurant, coffee bar, a heritage visitor attraction and a large flexible display and meeting area. This area was to be named The Forum.

Right from the agreement to proceed, the Director of Libraries was keen to ensure that the library reflected changes in customer expectations of libraries, and modern marketing planning techniques were employed to ensure a sound basis for communicating the messages, benefits and values of the new library. This was an ideal opportunity to transform the library from a solid and reliable, yet perhaps dull, service to a vibrant, outgoing, lively destination of choice, geared up to compete with its fast-paced retail neighbours.

How did Norfolk County Council Library and Information Service approach marketing the new library?

The underlying marketing planning assumptions for the new library with its associated services were:

- No honeymoon period. In retail markets there is always a short positive effect on trade when an outlet is refitted or an image updated. This honeymoon period does not always last and refits need to be undertaken on a regular basis. Given the relatively small amounts of marketing expenditure available to libraries, and certainly not enough for regular refits, it was decided to plan this introduction based on the need to avoid a honeymoon period.
- Do not steal from branches. The central library was to be marketed within an overall plan for the library service as a whole to stress the positive aspects of the existing branch network as well as the new resource.
- Be more businesslike in planning. Hence the tentative use of marketing planning tools such as the Ansoff matrix (see Chapter 6) to ensure both existing and potential new users were part of the plan.
- Segment the market then create marketing communications. There was a clear recognition that marketing would have to be highly targeted and based upon a detailed segmentation by benefits, rather than simply library functionality.

What did Norfolk County Library and Information Service do?

In the year before opening the new library a marketing communications campaign was implemented under the theme 'Just Imagine'. Sub-themes were 'computers @ your local library', 'stimulate your senses', 'picture Norfolk', 'libraries for learners' and 'performance sets'. A consultant was employed to define the logo and another was retained to develop media relations. However, consultants were used sparingly and much of the activity was devised and implemented by the library staff. This marketing planning, although in support of the new library, was part of a county-wide approach.

Given that the library is a major community resource it was decided to involve specific priority groups from the beginning. The design of the children's library, for instance, had a significant input from the children at a local middle school. An artist went into the school to capture the 'feel' the children described when discussing what a great library would be to them. The school was also given a sum of money to choose books for the new library.

The market had been segmented into four categories by attitude to enable the identification of quick wins. This segmentation, based upon work undertaken in arts marketing by Keith Diggle, identified attenders, intenders, the indifferent and the hostile as potential groups. A message was developed for each of these. Two categories (attenders, intenders) were chosen as the quick wins and formed the basis for the pre-opening push. The other two categories were developed further post-opening.

A key ally was the local press. A matrix was created to ensure the benefits for each of the segments were clear for both the Millennium Library and the branch libraries. All publicity was focused on key benefits and directed at specific user groups. This preparation of a series of messages meant that the library was always ready with a response for the media. The media came looking for stories and found that the library had a story, was ready to comment and would respond quickly.

Having ensured that the messages were ready it was essential to make sure that the promise in the message would be delivered in full. At the same time as the 'Just Imagine' campaign was introduced the library offer was also being developed. The staff person specification was changed to reflect a more diverse approach, and the softer human factors such as friendliness and approachability became more important in evaluating potential members of staff. To further reflect the friendly and helpful image being developed, library procedures, such as requirements for membership, were simplified. Attitudes within the library changed to actively look for ways to help readers around procedures, rather than find reasons for non-compliance with rules.

Given that the whole atmosphere and approach of the library were about to change from a rule-based organization to a customer-led organization, funds were made available for an extensive training programme to equip the staff to implement the intentions for the new library. This included sending a number of staff to the local college to learn about how people learn. All were trained in customer service. In this context customer service was not simply smiling at users but more about empowering staff to do what was right for the customer. Having sent out many messages via the media which suggested big changes were happening in the library service, it was important that when users arrived in the new library they did not find it to be just as it was.

In the weeks leading up to the opening of the new library, stories were drip-fed to the media about specific services. For a week before opening a desk was placed outside the new building which further built the excitement by tempting users to join before the library was open. This proved very successful, with a large number of pre-opening enrolments.

When all was in place and the new library was opened, a key marketing planning activity was to monitor closely what actually happened against target. Performance indicators were monitored monthly and deviations from forecast discussed.

In the first few weeks thousands of comments forms were collected. Most were supportive, offering ideas on potential improvements. A decision had been taken to react quickly to these comments and many small, yet significant, changes were made. A close watch has been maintained on comments forms, and it is noticeable that in recent times comments and suggestions have moved away from the general to the specific. It is now more likely to receive suggestions about specific items to be added to stock, rather than comments about the layout and atmosphere in the library.

Given that non-users might need to be persuaded to try the library, a series of incentives such as 'join now and get a free video loan' were offered.

What worked well?

Key user group targets were attracted as planned. Particularly successful was the campaign to attract parents and toddlers – 'baby rhyme time' sessions now regularly attract over 70 parents and babies. Teenagers, often not thought to be an easy target, became regular users of the library. The message to them was simple – free broadband internet access. There was no need to explain the richness of the library's book collection to entice them in, so this was not part of the marketing message. The environment looked right – a modern building with a Pizza Express and the potential for skateboarding in front of the library!

All of this has been sustained and the marketing planning has ensured that the library has prospered beyond the introductory period. Furthermore, visits and issues in other parts of the county do not appear to have suffered as a result of the new library in the major centre of population. The library has now been integrated into the service-wide marketing priorities which currently focus on families, ethnic minority groups, emergent readers and young men. Specific messages are being developed for these user groups based on the benefits they can receive from the library service, not just the resources available.

As this was a county-wide initiative it was important that results were general. There was increased use at all libraries. Active users increased from 20% in 2000 to 26% in 2003. Visits increased from 4.58 per head in 2000 to 5.6 in 2003. In 2003/4 the Norwich and Norfolk Millennium Library emerged as the busiest library in the English shire counties, issuing 875,334 books during the year – an improvement on third place in 2002/3 with issues of 859,679. Visits increased from a little over 1 million in 2002/3 to 1.1 million in 2003/4 and an impressive 1.4 million in 2004/5 and 1.5 million in 2006/6.

Although marketing planning cannot claim to be solely responsible for such growth, it is certainly considered by the Head of Libraries to be a major contributor.

What didn't work quite so well?

Although marketing has been a general success for the library, the success in attracting new user groups has meant that resources have not always been available to develop services for existing customers. In addition it has proved difficult to provide the atmosphere which combines both fun and excitement with a quiet centre of excellence study area.

Marketing the Norfolk and Norwich Millennium library in the future

The future is to market the library as part of the whole service. However, given the nature of its high profile as part of The Forum, the library is often the natural starting point for events and exhibitions which can then travel around the county's libraries. The Head of Libraries believes the Norfolk and Norwich Millennium Library is one of the best marketing tools the county library service has – it is always high profile by its very nature and can provide the talking point for informing and reminding users and non-users about similar collections (e.g. DVDs and CDs) throughout the county.

New marketing efforts are likely to be even more clearly focused on distinct segments. More marketing attention is being given to serving the daily incoming population. Efforts are being made to attract the large working population by stressing the benefits of popping into the library at lunchtime. Again, this is based on benefits rather than simple statements of available stock and other resources. The benefits, classic marketing, are associated with convenience and not eating into much-valued evening leisure time.

Key learning points for marketing planning in libraries

- start planning well in advance
- involve the community from the beginning
- make sure the staff are ready to deliver your planned changes
- always remember the impacts your marketing may have; success in one area should not damage other areas
- balance user-acquisition and retention-marketing planning activities
- marketing is not posters and promotions alone, but a more reflective planned process
- advertising libraries is about selling a lifestyle, not simply your services and resources.

Quick progress

Will your political masters wait three years for your strategic marketing plan to be implemented in full? Given the constantly changing agendas characteristic of local authorities, there is considerable pressure to remain tactical and allow seemingly longer-term strategies to wither. One way to guarantee continued commitment is to ensure quick progress with real outcomes and impacts at certain milestones within the planning period.

Look for 'quick wins' to sustain the energy in your marketing planning process

Many of the ideas in this book and toolkit require detailed reflective thinking. The benefits which will accrue from some of this activity are not likely to be immediate. In the business world it often takes three years of marketing planning before the system becomes truly embedded in the way planning is undertaken in an organization. In year one there is the disturbance to the 'normal' way of doing thing and the debilitating realization that our information base for planning is not as good as it should be. When this shock has been met and current limitations noted, the first year of detailed marketing planning will run into a second year where, although there will be indications that the organization is beginning to learn more about itself and its customers, some will question the value of detailed marketing planning. Wouldn't it have been better just to improve displays and mass market through advertising and promotional campaigns? It is at this point that the marketing planner needs to point to 'quick wins' that have been delivered as part of the planning process. 'Quick wins' are ideas that can be accomplished in a relatively short time, without great expense and with a positive outcome

Detailed reflection does not mean however, that there are not immediate benefits to be won from strategic marketing planning. On the contrary, best practice strategic marketing planning is always looking for a balance of short-term quick wins and long-term effective strategic positioning.

This balancing of both short- and long-term wins in public library strategic marketing is very important. On the one hand there is the constant round of new central government initiatives and local authority priorities which demands results within the one-year plan. On the other hand there is the underlying health of the public library service to consider – that part of the library service which will always exist independent of the current initiative. Without a strategic marketing approach to this the very core could wither away, leaving a financially challenged service when the funding for the current initiative dries up.

The branch library as a source of 'quick wins'

Quick wins can usually be made at branch library level. Although the small branch library has very little time and money available compared with service-wide initiatives, it usually has, through its staff, a close relationship with the community. Given that we have mentioned several times already the importance of viral marketing and recommendation as a key marketing activity, it is clear that branch library staff should not think of marketing as something that is done only by headquarters. Headquarters may create the value propositions and offers, and it may commission the advertisements on the sides of public transport and develop the library stories which appear on the radio. In spite of all this, it cannot convert the marketing activity into consistent issues, visits or enquiries unless the staff who interface with the public are true salespeople for the service.

Here are some of the reasons why branch libraries can undertake excellent marketing activity on a small budget.

1   Branch library staff are likely to be from the community and are able to build up trust within the user base. If the librarian recommends a book then this is often similar to being recommended a book by a trusted friend. Think about it. Would you buy a new domestic appliance simply on the basis of the advertisement and publicity material sent through your door, or would you be more influenced by a recommendation from a friend who had bought a particular make or model? Although your needs may not be exactly the same as your friend's you would certainly value their opinion and experience. The public library should be actively encouraging this relationship between users and branch library staff.

2   Many librarians are known by community leaders and will find it easy to gain invitations to speak at events or support events with collections of books and other materials. Again, being of the community rather than a representative to the community is a very powerful way to gain access to key people to convince them of your authenticity and value to the community.

3   Branch library staff can often spot the really important factor in studying a community which goes beyond the community profiling templates adopted by a headquarters management team. Headquarters may have co-ordinated the compilation of the community profile, but branch library staff will be able to go far beyond the neat and tidy quantifications such profiles usually offer. At corporate level these profiles are very useful to test things such as market penetration; at branch library level the staff may be able to highlight key factors not brought out by the statistics. For instance, in some areas people will,

for cultural reasons, be reluctant to cross a particular road within a notional library catchment area.

Marketing is not simply about large, expensive campaigns. It is about ensuring the basic infrastructure is right so that when the marketing message works the promise is delivered. Until the promise is delivered marketing remains ineffective. Branch library staff deliver the promise.

For quick wins it is important to ensure that the library is an inviting place to be. Do not spend significant intellectual and monetary resources on creating an excellent offer for particular segments only for those targeted to be disappointed the very first time they decide to try to claim the offer the library has made them. If users have to break down barriers your potential quick wins are lost. Rather than being tempted deeper into the library experience users may peek round the library door and decide it is not for them, even though the marketing communications messages they received seemed to be tempting.

Before rolling out any marketing initiative, challenge yourself, with the needs and wants of the specific user segment in mind.

- Is the library friendly, welcoming, and free of physical and psychological barriers?
- Is the layout attractive, with space? Have we employed the most appropriate layout and design elements from retail space planning?
- Does the signage help people to understand the way the library operates, or does it just add confusion? Do the users understand the words we use? Or are they just library jargon?
- Will the staff greet all users, from whatever background, with a genuinely friendly approach? We all have our own favourite human characteristics, but are staff committed to be responsive not just to their own favourite types of human beings but all users?
- Is everything clean and in good repair? It is no good sending out marketing messages about, say, access to the internet, if our public access computers either do not work or are unattractive.
- Does the library website have a logical layout which enables visitors to find the information they are seeking quickly?

If you cannot answer yes to each and every one of these key questions then you are in serious danger of destroying all of your hard strategic marketing planning activity for a lack of attention to detail. Any quick wins will be lost.

Using success stories

Another way to achieve quick wins is to piggyback on the success of others. With care it is possible to replicate the successful marketing activity of other library authorities. While each library authority serves a different local community there is some degree of similarity between many authorities. Look for success stories, consider what made them successful, and, where you feel there are similar circumstances in your own authority, do not be afraid to use those same ideas. However, simply copying other people will not guarantee success for you. Circumstances may have been slightly different in other authorities, so you do need to be careful.

Help is at hand to identify these potential sources of quick wins. There are a large number of organizations and websites which can help with effective marketing of libraries. Some are shown in the box below.

Online marketing information

- The Publicity and Public Relations Group of the Chartered Institute of Library and Information Professionals (UK) at www.cilip.org.uk/groups/pprg/: as well as details of public library and publicity awards, a selection of papers from past group conferences is available to download, including success stories; the group also holds courses, and produces publications and a newsletter
- @yourlibrary, at https://cs.ala.org/@yourlibrary/: the American Library Association's Campaign for America's Libraries, offering a good range of tools and materials; this site has a wealth of resources from printable artwork and sample press materials to quotable quotes about the value of libraries
- Information Today, Inc. - *Marketing Library Services*, at www.infotoday.com/MLS/: a very useful periodical on the subject and well worth a subscription; even if you do not subscribe there are some free articles at the website which cover very useful and practical topics

(Continued on next page)

- Gale: Free Resources – Market Your Library, at www.gale.com/free_ resources/marketing/find_yourself/: creative and marketing literature under the programme heading 'Find Yourself in the Library', with a variety of bookmarks and other templates available to download
- Marketing the Library, at www.oclc.org/marketing/: web-based training for public libraries, with six self-paced library marketing training modules, links to marketing resources, examples, quizzes and exercises
- Marketing Your Library, at www.librarysupportstaff.com/marketinglibs. html: an excellent selection of links to sites for marketing library services
- Marketing: Sources, at http://dis.shef.ac.uk/sheila/marketing/sources. htm: a little out of date now, but still a good source of links for any public librarian looking to develop their understanding of the applications of marketing ideas to their services.

Testing ideas

Good marketers are always undertaking small-scale experiments to test ideas. Consider introducing a small-scale experiment process where you can try things out and by looking closely at results identify quick wins. While it is preferable to base service developments on evidence of need, there are times when evidence collection may be slower and significantly more expensive than an experiment. Experiments need not be high profile and can be undertaken without publicity. Try a few low-issue books in your next display, for example. Or what happens if you make a sudden announcement that for the next hour every reader is allowed to borrow CDs at half price?

Performance targets

Many library authorities will look for quick wins to address quickly an apparent shortfall in meeting a performance target for visits or issues. Quick wins in this area include asking branch library staff to check with readers being issued their books whether they have found all that they looked for. If one in ten readers has not, then the library staff intervention could have an immediate impact on issues figures. Do the calculation. If your library has 500 book-borrowers a day and you can generate one extra borrowing from as few as one in ten borrowers on each borrowing occasion, then you may generate 50 extra issues per day, perhaps up to 300 extra issues per week, and 15,000 extra issues per year. Surveys suggest that there are indeed a number of readers who leave without getting all they came in for, so a friendly intervention by branch library staff to simply ask readers as they present for book issues whether or not they found everything they wanted may deliver a quick win. This intervention is highly targeted marketing in sympathy with the principles highlighted in the early part of this book.

Staffing for marketing planning and its implementation

It is increasingly common to see public library organization charts which include a marketing officer or similar. Establishing such a post shows commitment to marketing, and provides the resources to ensure implementation of projects. In many cases these posts are simply promotions officers responsible for running events or ensuring the local implementation of a national book industry or similar promotional event. This is very useful, but having read so far in this book you will doubtless be aware that this alone will not implement marketing planning throughout the public library system.

Often such posts are junior or at best middle-management posts which do not have access to the policy-making process which effective strategic marketing planning needs. Such planning needs to be undertaken by the senior management team as a whole and should be an ongoing agenda item for meetings of that team. It may be wise to appoint a marketing planning champion within the team. This person can ensure that the issues around marketing planning do not fall off the agenda. This person cannot, however, be expected to shoulder the responsibility for marketing planning: that is a senior management team responsibility. The real home for marketing planning in a public library is in a written standing agenda item, not in a job title.

In order to provide appropriate staffing for strategic marketing planning in your public library it will help to consider Table 8.1 (overleaf) as a contribution towards your wider competencies framework.

Table 8.1 Marketing planning competences for public libraries

Level	Role and contribution	Key skills
Senior management team	Devise and revise the marketing plan Secure and distribute resource for implementation Monitor implementation	Marketing planning skills Influencing skills
Middle and junior management , e.g. • promotions officer • relationship manager • marketing information manager	Manage implementation Allocate resources Report success, opportunities and constraints Deliver the promise, by user segment	Relationship development skills Project management skills
Library assistants	Deliver the promise via service points Report success, opportunities and constraints	People skills (developing customer relationships at service point level)

Whether or not you have specific marketing posts or not is unlikely to be the major factor in the quality of your marketing planning and implementation. Marketing is an orientation and it is likely that different library authorities will be able to achieve that orientation via different routes. For some the establishment of a named post will be culturally right; for others where marketing is naturally high profile there may not be a need for such a designated post.

Senior management and library assistants have very clear roles in marketing planning. The roles are not quite so clear at junior and middle management level. Here larger library systems will almost certainly need a promotions officer, as each promotion should be treated as a project with all the supporting project-management skills required. It is best practice not just to implement the promotional activity but will also monitor how successful or otherwise it has been. Notice that the title should be promotions officer and not marketing officer or similar. The author is aware of cases where public libraries have advertised for marketing officers, and appointed marketing professionals who have then been surprised and disappointed that the role is more promotional than marketing.

Other marketing-related options at junior and middle management include relationship managers for particular segments and marketing information managers to collect, analyse and present marketing-related information to the senior management team. You may already have a management information offer providing information on various performance indicators. Such a role could be adapted to include marketing information, which will not necessarily be the same as that provided to support reporting on performance measures and indicators.

A final word

Implementation of a strategic marketing plan rarely goes smoothly. Expect to make changes to your initial ideas, and prepare to react quickly when funding or other support for an existing initiative is suddenly withdrawn or when a new potential source of funding and support appears. This turbulence is natural and does not suggest that strategic marketing planning is a fruitless activity and ultimately a poor use of staff time. Indeed, if public libraries are to have a sound healthy base it is important to have a process in place which rides this turbulence, taking strength and quick wins from successive rounds of funding, while ensuring that the underlying mission vision and values of the public library service are constantly re-emphasized and marketed to the whole range of stakeholders. Strategic marketing planning is such a process. Strategy will always be part planned and part emergent.

This book has offered a practical and reflective approach to strategic marketing planning in public libraries. Plans that work are the result of a combination of clear thinking, sound decision-making, appropriate prioritization and excellent sustained implementation with a bias towards action. It is hoped that the tools and techniques in this book will inspire you to move from promotion to marketing, from one-year tactical plans to three-year strategic marketing plans. Happy planning!

Reflecting upon implementation of the marketing plan:

- Are you ready to reject frustration and disappointment when things do not go as planned?
- Have you communicated the plan to all stakeholders and secured their commitment to it?
- Is your action plan resourced?
- Have you ensured some small, highly likely 'quick wins' as part of the plan?
- Will you spot success when it happens and celebrate?
- Are you having fun?
- Have you switched the office light off after working long into the night on your marketing plan implementation?

Appendix

Twenty fast-track templates

These templates are available for download at
www.facetpublishing.co.uk/strategicmarketingplans/.

The following sequence of templates is not a substitute for reading the previous chapters. Templates adapted from the main text are presented here. If you have considered each of these areas in depth and are able to fill in the templates then you will have the raw material for a good marketing plan to be formatted in a way appropriate for your authority.

The templates help structure responses to the following key questions which arise during strategic marketing planning:

- Is the ambition clear? (A.1)
- Who is the user? (A.2)
- What are the key user requirements by segment? (A.3)
- Who, and how strong, are the competitors? (A.4)
- What factors will influence users and competitors over the coming planning period? (A.5)
- Is there a practical user segmentation? (A.6)
- Is there a value proposition for each segment? (A.7)
- Have strengths, weaknesses, opportunities and threats been identified? (A.8)

- Have all marketing strategy options been mapped? (A.9)
- Are priorities realistic? Can the chosen segments be won? (A.10)
- Given decisions on priorities (Chapter 5) and initial ambition (Chapter 2), what are the final marketing objectives? (A.11)
- Is there a strategy to manage stakeholders during the marketing planning process? (A.12)
- Have service development options been considered in terms of products to market? (A.13)
- Has an offer been developed for each segment? (A.14)
- Will users have a positive experience of the library service? (A.15)
- Is there a set of general and segment-specific messages for users and non-users? (A.16)
- Is there a set of marketing communications that can be used for both general marketing and segment-specific activity? (A.17)
- Is there a detailed action plan with timescales and responsibilities allocated? (A.18)
- Is there a resource plan to implement the marketing plan? (A.19)
- Given that things will almost certainly not go as planned, has the plan identified the major risks to manage? (A.20)

Is the ambition clear?

Vision: What? The picture of the future we hope to create	
Mission: How will we move towards the vision in the medium term?	
Values: How do we want to act, consistent with our mission, along the path toward achieving our vision?	
Quantified ambition: Issues, visits, enquiries, etc., now and in three years' time	

Figure A.1   Statement of ambition

Who is the user?

Library product, service or offer	Customer (person who makes the decision on the use of the library)	Consumer (person who actually uses the library)	Influencer (person who influences use of the library)

Figure A.2   Distinguishing customers and consumers

What are the key user requirements by segment?

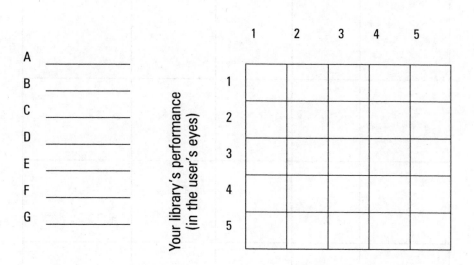

Importance to user segment

A _____
B _____
C _____
D _____
E _____
F _____
G _____

Figure A.3   An importance/performance matrix

Who, and how strong, are the competitors?

Library product, service or offer	Competitor	Competitors' strengths in this area	Competitors' weaknesses in this area	Our relative position compared with competitors'

Figure A.4   How strong is the library offer when compared with competitor offers?

What factors will influence users and competitors over the coming planning period?

	Anticipated changes and events during planning period	Effects on user and non-user groups (does it make them more or less likely to need or use library services?)	Effects on competitors (does it make them weaker or stronger?)	Implications for library service
Political				
Economic				
Social				
Technological				
Legislative				
Environmental				

Figure A.5   Public library PESTLE

Is there a practical user segmentation?

We see our library market breaking down into the following segments	What are our products and services for this segment?	How will we reach this segment?	How will this segment help us to achieve our ambition?
Segment A			
Segment B			
Segment C			

Figure A.6   A practical user segmentation

Is there a value proposition for each segment?

Benefit user group/segment is looking for	
Why use a library to get that?	
Why use a library rather than an alternative? (differential benefit)	

Figure A.7   Creating a value proposition (one or more per segment)

Have strengths, weaknesses, opportunities and threats been identified?

Strengths	Weaknesses
Opportunities	**Threats**

Figure A.8   SWOT analysis

Have all marketing strategy options been mapped?

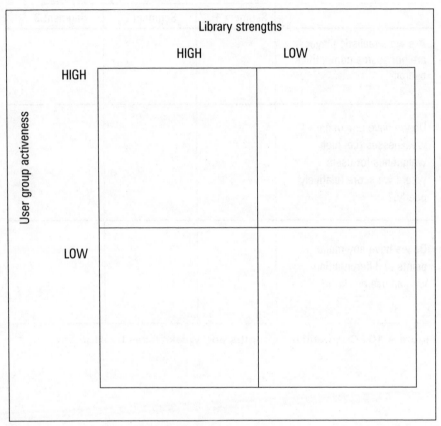

Figure A.9 Directional policy matrix

Are priorities realistic? Can the chosen segments be won?

	Segment 1	Segment 2	Segment 3
Are we a realistic player – are our scores competitive overall?			
Do we have any major weaknesses (i.e. high weightings for users where we score relatively poorly)?			
Do we have any major points of differentiation we can use as USPs?			

Figure A.10 Competitive strengths and weaknesses by segment

Given decisions on priorities (Chapter 5) and our initial ambition (Chapter 2), what are the final marketing objectives?

	T	T+1	T+2	T+3
Issues				
Visits				
Enquiries				
Website hits				
Other				

Figure A.11 Objectives by segment or service-wide

Is there a strategy to manage stakeholders during the marketing planning process?

Key stakeholder	Stakeholder's interest in the marketing strategy	Stakeholder's influence on the implementation of marketing strategy: positive or negative?	Strategy to manage the stakeholder

Figure A.12   Stakeholder analysis

Have service development options been considered in terms of products to market?

Offer (Products/services)

	Existing	New
Existing		
New		

Community group or segment

Figure A.13 Service development options

Has an offer been developed for each segment?

	Segment A	Segment B	Segment C
Product or service			
Price, or costs reduced for user/non-user			
Key ways to access the product or service (place)			
Promotional activity			
Politics			
Partners in the offer and their contribution			
Relationships strategy (How close to the segment are we? How close do we want to be?)			

Figure A.14 The library offer to specific segments

Will users have a positive experience of the library service?

	What response do we want from users?	Will they naturally make this response?	If 'yes', how can we enhance the experience? If 'no', how can we make it 'yes'?
Feel			
Sense			
Think			
Do			

Figure A.15 Managing the user's experience

Is there a set of general and segment-specific messages for users and non-users?

General messages to users and non-users	Segment-specific messages to users and non-users
1 2 3	Segment A 1 2 3 Segment B 1 2 3 Segment C 1 2 3

Figure A.16 Create a set of marketing messages

Is there a set of marketing communications that can be used for both general marketing and segment-specific activity?

	General interest	Segment-specific
Stock marcoms		
Event-specific marcoms		

Figure A.17 Ensuring an appropriate set of marketing communications

Is there a detailed action plan with timescales and responsibilities allocated?

Segment A	Action	Timescale	Resource	Responsibility

Objective: ————
   Strategies:
    1. ————
 	
   2. ————				

Figure A.18 Example action plan

Is there a resource plan to implement the marketing plan?

Activity	Direct costs	Indirect costs	Total cost of activity

Figure A.19 Resource requirement

Given that things will almost certainly not go as planned, has the plan identified the major risks to manage?

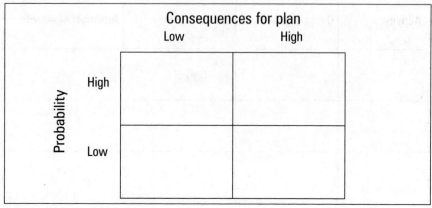

Figure A.20   A risk matrix

Select bibliography

There is a wealth of literature on strategic marketing planning in both book and article form. If you are inspired to read more on the topic the following books are particularly recommended.

Process of marketing planning

Kotler, Philip, and Keller, Kevin (2005) *Marketing Management*, 12th edn, New Jersey, Prentice Hall. ISBN: 0 1314 5757 8.

> The world's best-selling title on marketing management, now with a more detailed look at brand management.

McDonald, Malcolm (2002) *Marketing Plans: how to prepare them, how to use them*, 5th edn, Oxford, Butterworth Heinemann. ISBN: 0 7506 5625 5.

> By the author of other marketing books on services marketing and retail marketing, but this is the classic. If you read one other book on marketing planning it should be this one. Practical and thoughtful.

Piercy, Nigel (2002) *Market-led Strategic Change: a guide to transforming the process of going to market*, 3rd edn, Oxford, Butterworth Heinemann. ISBN: 0 7506 5225 X.

> Packed with case-study examples and written in a very relaxed, engaging style.

Strategic marketing planning in libraries

This book has tried to remain very practical. However, the tools and techniques offered are based upon current marketing concepts and ideas. The following two scholarly texts will provide the public librarian with a very well referenced overview of some key marketing concepts as they might apply to library services.

Owens, Irene (2003) *Strategic Marketing in Library and Information Science*, Binghamton, NY, Haworth Press. ISBN: 0 7890 2142 0.

de Sáez, Eileen Elliott (2002) *Marketing Concepts for Libraries and Information Services*, 2nd edn, London, Facet Publishing. ISBN: 1 85604 426 2.

Index